Authentically Local

THE Fairmont KEA LANI MAUI

On the island of Maui, at the base of Haleakalā, and on the shore of the pristine Polo Beach, stands a luxury resort unlike any other. Striking white against the deep blue of the Pacific, The Fairmont Kea Lani, Maui nearly demands attention. With its all-suite accommodations, including exclusive 2 and 3-bedroom villas, a full service spa, three swimming pools and multiple dining and retail options, the resort is both unique and impressive. Yet with all this, The Fairmont Kea Lani still creates a personal and relaxed experience for its guests. This sincere and humble hospitality is indicative of Hawaiian culture; a culture that the colleagues at The Fairmont Kea Lani live and breathe every day.

Fairmont believes that hotels aren't simply placed throughout the world; they thrive as part of a community, sharing the customs and culture that make each location unique and interesting. The Fairmont Kea Lani is no different. Guests recognize the authenticity of the outrigger canoe experience, the 'ukulele lessons or the Hawaiian lei making class. And colleagues—the people at the heart of the resort—take the responsibility of perpetuating their culture with passion and sincerity. It isn't a show; it is a true and honest desire for visitors to leave Maui with a better understanding of the richness of Hawaiian culture.

The Fairmont Kea Lani is a remarkable resort nestled between the deep blue water of the Pacific and the lush foliage of Wailea. But it is more than a beautiful façade. It is a place full of passion, devotion and love for the spirit and culture of Hawai'i.

Celebrating Maui

In 2008, one of Maui's most popular and well-known chefs, Executive Chef Tylun Pang, gathered a team of passionate people at The Fairmont Kea Lani, to help him develop the newest Maui restaurant. At the time, there were (and still are) many top-notch restaurants in Maui. But Chef Pang wanted something different; something that truly captured the essence of Maui and perpetuated the culture of Hawai'i. Maui may be a small island, but it has a rich history and a fierce spirit. It's a place of cultural diversity, exquisite cuisine and an honest celebration for life. A place where community, friends, families and visitors, come together and are grateful for the beauty and heritage of the island. It's a place unlike any other in the world, and the team wanted to let everyone know.

It was a tall order to develop a restaurant that captured this uniqueness. First, they immersed themselves in Maui's roots, sharing historical books, photographs and stories of the people living on Maui over a hundred years ago. They turned to colleagues within the resort who had lived on Maui for years and who had treasured family recipes to share. They sourced the freshest local produce and identified the highest quality sustainable seafood and Maui-raised cattle. And they determined that if this restaurant was going to represent Maui, it had to be a meeting place—one where locals and visitors alike could come together and share stories, laughter and incredible cuisine. And each one could leave, not only with a full belly, but also with a new understanding of the island's rich history and cultural influence.

And So, Along Came Kō

Kō restaurant pays homage to the heritage of Maui and the many ethnicities that contributed to its culture. In 1828, the first sugar mill on Maui began its operations. The sugar industry grew rapidly, and so did its need for manpower, bringing people from around the world to the island. This created the "melting pot of the Pacific"—a group of hard-working immigrants who came together to share food, spices, and culinary techniques. This blend of ethnicities, Hawaiian, Chinese, Filipino, Portuguese, Korean, and Japanese is certainly reflected on the Kō menu, but even more so, has influenced and shaped Maui's unique and spirited culture.

Kō is more than a tribute to the people of the past; it's also a nod to Maui's people of today. Kō represents the many farmers that drive the freshest local produce down the slopes of Haleakalā each morning, the fishermen who brave the north shore swell in the winter to get the best seafood and the business owners, partners, and people throughout the community who share and support Fairmont's commitment to local ingredients and sustainable seafood. Kō is reflective of the seasoned bartenders and servers, who share Maui's culture each night with sharp knowledge and sincere pride. Kō is found in the culinary team, led by Chef Pang at The Fairmont Kea Lani, who has contributed family recipes and preparation techniques to the menu that have been passed down for generations.

Chef Pang serves many of the recipes in this book at Kō each night. The menu offers innovative dishes made with simple and fresh ingredients, yet remarkably result in complex and unique flavors. Yes, the food is phenomenal and people, both local and visiting, love it. But what truly makes the experience at Kō come alive is everything that went into it: the stories, the people, the history, the food, and the passion of Maui. That's Kō.

For more information about The Fairmont Kea Lani or Kō restaurant, visit www.fairmont.com/kealani or call 808-875-4414.

What Maui
LIKES TO EAT™

What Maui
LIKES TO EAT™

By

Tylun Pang

What Maui
LIKES TO EAT ™

By
Tylun Pang

with
Gail Ainsworth

Photography by
Kaz Tanabe

Mutual Publishing

Library of Congress Cataloging-in-Publication Data

Pang, Tylun.
    What Maui likes to eat / by Tylun Pang ; with Gail Ainsworth.
       p. cm.
    Includes bibliographical references and index.
    ISBN 1-56647-936-3 (hardcover : alk. paper)
    1. Hawaiian cooking. 2. Cooking--Hawaii--Maui. 3. Cookbooks.
I. Ainsworth, Gail. II. Title.

    TX724.5.H3P35 2010
    641.59969'21--dc22

                    2010035322

ISBN-10: 1-56647-936-3
ISBN-13: 978-1-56647-936-3

Design by Courtney Young

First Printing, October 2010
Second Printing, October 2011

Mutual Publishing, LLC
1215 Center Street, Suite 210
Honolulu, Hawai'i 96816
Ph: 808-732-1709 / Fax: 808-734-4094
email: info@mutualpublishing.com
www.mutualpublishing.com

Printed in China

All photography by Kaz Tanabe, except as indicated below.

Photos by Tylun Pang: pg. xv, 1, 8-9, 11, 21-22, 28, 37-38, 41, 44, 52, 55, 63 (background), 71, 81, 86, 96, 99, 101 (top), 106 (top), 107, 110, 113, 116, 121-122 (top), 127, 129, 131-132, 152, 171 (bottom), 220, 223 (top)

Photos from Dreamstime.com: pg. 5 © Ruben Paz, pg. 12 © Pipa100, pg. 14 (top) © Lepas, pg. 14 (bottom) © Paul Cowan, pg. 15 © Wikki, pg. 22 (bottom) © Elena Moiseeva, pg. 23 © Nataliya Evmenenko, pg. 42 (bottom) © Shawnhemp, pg. 56 © Le Do, pg. 58, 62 © Shariff Che' Lah, pg. 59 © Norman Chan, pg. 63 (left) © Michael Rolands, pg. 63 (right) © Timothy Lee, pg. 65, 146 © Vasiu, pg. 70 © Mailthepic, pg. 83 © Ramon Grosso, pg. 84 © Mchudo, pg. 92, 111 © Ippeito, pg. 93 © Andrzej Tokarski, pg. 95 © Angel Luis Simon Martin, pg. 101 (bottom) © Sally Scott, pg. 114 (right) © Zaxstar, pg. 117 © Rimantas Abromas, pg. 136 © Vitaly Vasin, pg. 143 © Ockra, pg. 151 (bottom) © Bddigitalimages, pg. 152 (bottom) © Fedor Kondratenko, pg. 154 (photo paper) © Ewanthot, pg. 156 © Mcarrel, pg. 202 © Showmethemoney, pg. 219 © Elena Babushkina, pg. 227 © Slallison

Photos courtesy of Gail Ainsworth: pg. xiii, 238 (bottom)
Photos courtesy of Henry & Judy Silva: pg. 43, 216-217
Photo © Douglas Peebles: pg. 51
Photo © Nina Lee: pg. 135 (Chef Bev Gannon)
Photo © Steve Brinkman: pg. 142 (Chef Ryan Luckey)
Photo © Ka'anapali Beach Hotel: pg. 151 (Chef Tom Muromoto)
Photos courtesy of (or material provided by) the Mizoguchi family pg. 156, 158 (top), 161 (bottom); Sonny Gamponia pg. 157, 164, 178; the Kametani family pg. 158 (bottom), 168; the Lee family: pg. 159; the Watanabe family: pg. 160, 161 (top); Robert Santos: pg. 162, 176, 179; Jackie Pias Carlin: pg. 163; Robbie St. Sure Lum: pg. 165; Morlee Walters: pg. 166 (top); Bonnie Tuell: pg. 166 (bottom); Louise Martelles: pg. 167; Hāli'imaile Pineapple Company pg. 171; Robert Lu'uwai pg. 172; DePonte family pg. 180; Lorraine Fujiyama pg. 181 (top); Alec Probst pg. 181 (bottom); Johnny Valera pg. 182; Harold Sambrano pg. 184; Wayne Tanaka pg. 185; Carlene Laughlin pg. 186; Nancy Kawaharada Shimoda pg. 188; Alvin and Midge Cheee pg. 189; the Kitada family pg. 190; Hugh Starr pg. 192; Barbara Long pg. 193; Charlene Hokama pg. 194, 197; Darrell Orwig pg. 195
Photo © The Maui News: pg. 191
Photo © The Maui Historical Society: pg. 196

Contents

Plantation-Inspired Cuisine

Grown on Maui

Guest Chefs

Community Recipes

PŪPŪ AND SNACKS

SALADS

ENTRÉES

SIDE DISHES

DESSERTS

MISCELLANEOUS

Restaurants Gone By

Sweet Maui Endings

Acknowledgments

I'm grateful for the opportunity to acknowledge those dear individuals who have been my inspiration and my support, helping me become the chef I am today.

Let me start at the beginning with my Dad, Yun Young Pang, and both of my grandmothers Ah E Popo See Moi Chun and Mary Yuen, all from whom I inherited my love of cooking. And of course, my Mom, Mili "Eat Dessert First" Pang, from whom I inherited my love of food and who believes that the world is at your fingertips, all you have to do is grab it!

Then there's my darling wife and best friend, Mary-Jo Pang, who always supports me, takes care of our family and holds down the fort while I'm at work and lets me use her kitchen when I am finally at home at mealtime; Herbert and Fusae Lim, Mary-Jo's parents and my biggest fans—thanks for always being there; my son who always makes me proud, Timothy Pang—cooking for his athletic teams and competitions has enabled me to perfect large portion potluck kid food; my dearest daughters who I adore, Malia King, Moani Borge, Miki'ala King, and my grandson, Slayder King-Fernandez.

My sisters and their families have always been supportive of my cooking, giving me excellent feedback; Robert & Jody Domingo, Robb, Claire, Kahikinaokala Tylun, Kaiao, Kauha'anui and Keaolamalamaokahikilani Ku'ikahi Domingo, Bryce & Tammy and Kalepono Domingo, Starr and Jordon Makana Domingo, Joy, Kelin and Khaya Domingo, Halona Felix, Liana Pang and Randi Tamura, Raymond & Tami Orozco, Melisa & Francisco Vargas, Raymi & John Michael Faria, Travis Orozco, Sepia, Momotaro, Sadie, Cleo, Dennis & Mari, Mia, Christopher & Evie Joy Chan, Mitchell & Crystal, Maianna and Kason Pinzon. Warmest aloha to my nephew Mason Chan who inspired our entire family to "LIVE STRONG." You are always in our hearts!

Farrant, who takes care of Mili, Rick & Burt Chung, what would we do without you?

The chefs who taught me along the way include Chef Reiner Greubel, Chef Siegbert Wendler, and Hans Weiler. Their guidance and support have stayed with me throughout my culinary career.

Colleagues from The Fairmont Kea Lani, Maui who helped with the book or provided background support include Christof Luedi, Mahealani Youn, Wendy Harvey, Pete Sylvester, April Storey, Chef Richard Ramirez, Chef Richard Hoang, Rick Texeira, George Agcolicol, Marilyn Mina, Aristotle Aurelio, Linda Axe, Shawn Cabania, Sean Ribucan, Eduardo Domingo, Wilson Villalba, Gerry Famorca, Jeffrey Ang, Jackie Brown, Shane Tomas, Eric Dela Cruz, Ricky De Boer, Olivier Carlut, Amber Fontanilla, Melodee Mataele, Constante Garcia, Colleen Chong, and Jody Joaquin.

I was fortunate to receive support and encouragement from my culinary peers, friends, and fellow chefs as they generously contributed their time and treasured recipes. Chris Speere (Maui Culinary Academy); John and Vicktoria Keanaaina (Valley Isle Seafood); Nelson Okumura, Kyle Mainaga, and Paula Rafanan (VIP Foodservice); Kenny Sinclair, Bargreen Ellingson, Charlene Kauhane (Kauhane Communications); Becky Speere (Maui Cattle Company); Chancy Monden (Kula Country Farms); Bryan Otani (Bryan Otani Farms); Neil Nakamura (Triple N Farms); Craig Nihei (CN Farms); Thomas and Eva Kafsack (Surfing Goat Dairy); Toni Stanich (Ali'i Kula Lavender); Poncho Calibuso (Kula Produce Company); Walter Evonuk and Terry Chang (Evonuk Farms); Sam Choy; Mark Ellman; Perry Bateman; Tom Muromoto; Bev Gannon; Ryan Luckey; Geno Sarmiento; Ryan Funasaki, Beau Moore & Doug Wee (Tommy Bahama Wailea); Shibori by Burgundy; and Michael Miyashiro & Beverley Inoue (Rainforest).

The Mutual Publishing 'ohana were extremely helpful walking me step by step through the publishing process, which I never realized was so involved. Mahalo to Karen Lofstrom, Kaz Tanabe, Louis Latilla, Richard Ahn, Jane Gillespie, Sandie Hata, Alfred Monico, Jordan Padilla, Erika Roberts, Lynette Shimabukuro, Gay Wong and Courtney Young.

Gail Ainsworth prepared the chapters for Community Recipes and Restaurants Gone By after I hit a dead-end. Her network of friends, contacts, and Maui foodies was amazing. Gail, thanks for coming to the rescue.

And last, but not least, to the wonderful people of Maui who share their food knowledge and help make Maui a unique culinary place—the farmers that grow, the fishermen, the chefs and home cooks that buy local and eat fresh. Mahalo!

Tylun Pang

*H*aving the opportunity to think, talk, and write about Maui food and Maui restaurants of the past has been quite a pleasure. For those who were willing to share their stories, and for the photographs, menus and memorabilia which add immeasurably to the stories, I have a great number of people to thank.

First of all, gratitude goes to all the people associated with the restaurants, as owners, chefs, employees and their friends and relatives: Rhonda Lincoln, Gandy and Eric Molina, Ruth DePonte, Ruth Ann DePonte, Alec Probst, Lorraine and Linda Fujiyama, Mark and Sophie Whitehead, Johnny Valera, Alyce Carmichael, Harold Sambrano, Takashi and Kathy Toda, Carlene Laughlin, Nancy Kawaharada Shimoda, Midge and Alvin Chee, Shirley Chee, Ethel Kitada Hotema, Lorraine Kitada Takaoka, Eileen McDonald, Christa Conner, George Fukushima, Katherine D. Smith, John Otto and Hugh Starr.

For sharing their dining experiences and knowledge of local restaurants, I have the following to thank: Burt Sakata, Jackie Pias Carlin, Linda Decker, Bonnie Friedman, Robbie St. Sure Lum, Robert Santos, Ron Youngblood, Tom Stevens, Marilyn Umetsu, Harlan Hughes, Sophie Whitehead, Midge Chee, Sonny Gamponia, Rene Yamafuji, and Barbara Long. Thanks to Charlene Hokama, Darrell Orwig and Wayne Tanaka for photographs.

For their generosity in sharing local and family recipes, stories and photographs, I am most grateful to all the recipe contributors. In addition I would like to thank Marilyn Umetsu, Judy Muranaka, Yvonne Dias, Sonny Gamponia, Rodrigo Balala, Carol Kametani Nagano, Elizabeth Oishi, Robert Santos, Louie Rosado and Delores Bio, who helped me to obtain the recipes, stories and photographs. Also, I am indebted to all the family members who are no longer with us who passed their culinary heritage on to their children and grandchildren so that we all may share.

Although their names have already been mentioned above, I would particularly like to recognize my local food and restaurant consultants Marilyn Umetsu and Robert (Bobbie) Santos, who spent much time guiding me along my way. Hey you guys, let's go eat!

Aloha nō,
Gail Ainsworth

Introduction

My Early Days

I love cooking and sharing food with family and friends. It's a passion I inherited from my father and grandmothers. When I was a child, I always used to watch them cook. I was fascinated by everything in the kitchen and cooking itself—the stove, the pots and pans, cutting the food into pieces, dipping it in sauces, smelling the aromas. In those days, my family's mealtimes were special. The entire family sat down at the table. Everyone had their own seat. TV wasn't allowed. We ate, talked, and connected. Everything came from the kitchen—no take-out, no fast food.

I also loved tagging along with my dad and shopping in Oʻahu's Chinatown. It was all about seeing, smelling, touching, and tasting all the fresh foods that he needed to make his famous Gon Lo Mein. Even today when I close my eyes I can still see Dad in the kitchen. Each time he cooked, he made the dish differently. The chicken and vegetables were easy, but the sauce was always a challenge! He'd measure all the ingredients ahead of time, fire up the wok, and start experimenting. Eventually he got it just right—so ʻono!

Being surrounded by great home cooks like my dad and grandmas, it was no big surprise that my first job, in the summer after ninth grade, was at Kenny's Burger House at the Kam Shopping Center in Kalihi. Even though I mainly flipped burgers, I still learned that good cooking is about being precise and paying attention to detail—even for the simplest of dishes.

After graduating high school, I worked at the Ilikai Hotel in Waikīkī, completing a three-year culinary apprenticeship program for the State of Hawaiʻi and Westin Hotels. A requirement of the program was to learn the basics of the bakery. I learned that everything had to be weighed and measured exactly. (Thanks, Hans Wieler, for not giving up on me.) When I finished my training, I moved to Los Angeles, where I was an opening team member for the Los Angeles Bonaventure Hotel. The cuisine at that time was upscale and classical European, involving many steps, many layers, and long cooking times. (Today when I dine out, I always appreciate the dishes that take a long time to cook, because I know how much effort they require.)

Going to Maui

But I missed Hawai'i—including its local-style gatherings and lū'au with poke, potluck, and talk story. And most of all, I missed my dad and cooking old-time food with him. So I was happy to return to the Islands for a second tour of duty at the Ilikai Hotel, where I eventually became the executive chef for a few years before being transferred to Kaua'i and finally to Maui, where I've been living and cooking for the last fifteen years. Although I'm an O'ahu boy and I love all the islands, Maui truly has my heart, and my family enjoys calling this home. Maui is exciting and busy, but still has a great Island lifestyle. It has modern elements and conveniences, but you can still find the old-time places and the laid-back pace that we associate with an older Hawai'i. There are vibrant small towns such as Pā'ia, Makawao, and Wailuku, where you can walk down streets lined with shops and bakeries and small eateries. And I enjoy being able to buy just-picked produce from roadside stands or farmer's markets.

Maui has fabulous restaurants no matter what your tastes—from five-star dining rooms to hole-in-the-wall ethnic eateries. Sometimes the most 'ono food is sold out of the back of a truck! Maui's abundant small eateries are so enticing, I sometimes drive across the island just for a particular dish. The saimin, shave ice, and guri guri ice cream are well worth it! And the eateries are family-owned, emphasizing teamwork and pride. (I always like to hire people who worked in family businesses because they bring a certain know-how and pride to the job.)

The commonly heard proclamation "Maui Nō Ka 'Oi" *(Maui is the Best)* is truly applicable to the culinary scene here. Maui food draws from many traditions. When the missionaries brought Yankee cooking to the Islands, the Hawaiians created Westernized versions of their favorite dishes. Later, the contract workers from Asia and Europe who arrived to work on the plantation brought their own cuisines. At mealtimes, food was traded and shared. It was inevitable that recipes would be borrowed and mixed to create plantation fusion, leading to today's delicious and distinctive local cuisine. (You'll find several of these recipes in the Maui Kine Grindz chapter.) Of all the islands, Maui is the most influenced by plantation traditions. People are still working and living in plantation camps, growing their own crops, swapping recipes with their neighbors and their children. So much culinary energy is still coming from the plantation.

Maui cooking is about people. The more people pitch in, the better the food tastes! I use this philosophy in the Fairmont Kea Lani kitchen, where I ask my entire team

to share their ideas. Everyone exchanges recipes, tips, and best places to purchase ingredients. Everyone brings food to taste at work.

Maui food is also about culture. People like to eat what they grow up eating. It's memory food—people cooking what is close to them. Local food is all about our cultural ties. I make a point of learning about a culture before cooking new food. If you know how a food originated, and how it was originally cooked, you'll make it all the better, even though you may adjust and fine-tune the recipe. A Hawai'i hotel kitchen represents the ethnic composition of the Islands. Therefore, my kitchen staff are some of my best teachers.

It's exciting that young people are getting involved in the culinary scene. Enrollment has doubled at the Maui Culinary Academy, where, as a part of the advisory board, I'm involved in training more and more local chefs. These enthusiastic and professional newcomers bring great energy to our local food scene. Students know that they can have a culinary career at the Fairmont Kea Lani and other hotels and resorts, provided they are willing to work hard and can take long, demanding hours.

What makes our food on Maui so 'ono is the ingredients. Good food depends on fresh ingredients. It starts with the farms. Here on Maui many of our small farms have been run by the same family for generations. They know their land, their crops, and their growing cycles. Local fishermen and ranchers also carry on Hawaiian traditions. All our growers take tremendous pride in their produce.

I find it helpful to know the sources. I like to ask how or why farmers grew their crop, which fisherman brings in the best type of fish, where the sweetest fruit is grown. In Lahaina and Kīhei, for example, mangoes are sweetest due to the dryer weather; local fishermen know it's going to be a good moi season when mango flowers are abundant on the tree; and Hāna fishermen catch some of the best 'ahi. My purveyors keep me aware of the growing seasons, so I know what is available and what will taste especially good. Listening to the farmers and fishermen and their stories helps me understand what they produce and what's being caught. I can then use my knowledge and training to take the flavors to the next level. It's all about knowing and understanding what you are cooking.

My Cooking Style

I believe in respecting culture and in simplicity—serving the food as close to its natural state as possible, with fewer steps and fewer ingredients. It it's a fish dish, it should look and taste like a fish and remind you of the ocean from which it came.

I learned to cook Chinese and local food from my grandmothers and my dad. Later I learned to cook in the classical European and continental styles from the head chefs at the Los Angeles Bonaventure, Century Plaza, and Ilikai hotels. They were strict and demanding, which was necessary to prepare complex dishes, some of which took days to complete. As I've developed my own style of cooking, I've tried to combine local and European traditions.

Cooking to me should be spontaneous and fun. It should respect the integrity of the ingredients in the way the wok does. I grab a wok before any skillet. I love the wok because of its versatility—you can do anything in it. It's good for deep-frying, sautéing, stir-frying, and steaming. With a wok, dishes come together in a flash.

About the Book

This book represents my love affair with Maui food. My publisher was expecting Hawai'i Regional Cuisine recipes. And that's how I began. But after gathering, selecting, and editing, I ended up with more local-style recipes with my added twists. Several recipes we serve at Kō Restaurant at the Fairmont Kea Lani are inspired by the mix of cuisines from Hawai'i's plantation camp days.

To ensure that I was accurately representing Maui food, I turned to other Maui chefs who share my cooking philosophy. I also realized that a lot of good cooking is done privately, for family and friends, so I asked Gail Ainsworth to chase down what I call community recipes. Maui also has a strong tradition of dining out, and Gail, through her diligent research, was able to provide a fun tour of bygone restaurant days.

So what we end up with is Maui food as cooked and enjoyed by Mauians. All of these recipes are relatively easy to make. If you can't find the exact ingredients because you don't live on Maui, there should be reasonable substitutes available. I hope you enjoy creating these Maui recipes and that you will learn some interesting Maui tidbits in the process.

Plantation–Inspired Cuisine

Here in Hawai'i, many of us are descended from hard-working immigrants who came to the islands to work on the plantation and it's in our food, especially, that we feel their love and influence. The Fairmont Kea Lani has been avant garde in allowing their guests to experience plantation inspired cuisine in Kō Restaurant (Kō means "sugarcane" in Hawaiian) representing both our cultural and culinary heritage. The dishes served at the restaurant combine the different cuisines that were introduced by our fore bearers. The Hawaiians, for example, shared their method of cooking food underground in an imu; the Portuguese used stone ovens to make their sweet breads; the Chinese introduced rice and soy sauce; the Filipinos, pancit and adobo; the Japanese, simple steamed or boiled dishes. Many of these cooking methods—salting meat, pickling vegetables in vinegar, eating fish with horseradish—helped preserve food in the days before refrigeration. Here are recipes for lobster tempura, Kobe beef poke, chicken and shiitake mushroom lumpia, and many others that bring out the best in all our different cultures.

Zarzuela

A zarzuela is a Spanish operetta, combining dialogue, song, and dance. A zarzuela de marisco is a fish stew; like the operetta, it combines different elements to make a harmonious—and very tasty—whole.

Processed fresh from a good fish market is best, but quality frozen seafood can work. I prefer cold water lobster tails, Maine, Australian, or Tristan.

Frozen is more accessible. Most places that carry fresh products will most likely be able to process it for you. If using frozen seafood, it is best to defrost in the refrigerator before use.

It takes canny shopping to buy saffron that is both good and relatively inexpensive. Cook's Illustrated *recently did a study of saffron and recommended Penzeys as both good and inexpensive.*

This fish dish comes together quickly once you've done the prep.

Split the lobster tails in half, lengthwise; leave the meat in the shell.

Cut up the chorizo, onions, garlic, bell pepper, tomato, and green olives per the ingredients list.

Heat the olive oil in a large pot over medium-high heat. Add the onions, garlic, and bell peppers, and sauté for 4 minutes. Add the chorizo and continue cooking for 2 minutes. Next add the white wine, clam juice, and water. Then stir in the chopped tomatoes and the oregano, paprika, saffron, and bay leaf; simmer for 10 minutes. Season with the salt and pepper.

While the broth is simmering you can cut up lemons to make lemon wedges, and cut parsley into sprigs for garnish. I haven't suggested amounts; you're the best judge of how much garnish you and your family or guests would like.

Add the lobster and cover the pot; simmer for 3 minutes, then add the rest of the seafood and cover and simmer for approximately 2 minutes until done.

PRESENTATION

Fill 4 large bowls with stew; make sure that everyone gets some of each kind of seafood. Serve garnished with lemon wedges and parsley sprigs on the side.

Yield: 4 servings

2 (approximately 5 ounces each) lobster tails
12 (size 13/15) tiger prawns
12 (size 10/20) scallops
24 (2 dozen) Manila clams
12 mussels
¼ cup chopped chorizo sausage (½-inch chunks)
¼ cup diced Maui onion (½-inch dice)
1 tablespoon minced garlic
¼ cup diced red bell pepper (½-inch dice)
½ cup seeded and chopped tomato (use canned diced tomatoes if you can't find fresh tomatoes that you like)
12 green olives, cut in half
¼ cup olive oil
1 cup white wine
1½ cups clam broth
1½ cups water

1 teaspoon dried oregano
½ teaspoon paprika
½ teaspoon saffron
1 bay leaf
Salt and freshly ground pepper to taste

Lemon wedges and chopped parsley for garnish

Pancit Noodles

Yield: 4 servings

8 (13/15 size) frozen shrimp, peeled and deveined with head off
2 ounces sliced lup cheong (Chinese sausage)
½ cup thinly sliced Kula onions
¼ cup thinly sliced celery
¼ cup thinly sliced carrots
½ cup cabbage, sliced
4 tablespoons vegetable oil
1 teaspoon minced garlic
2 cups chicken broth
1 tablespoon oyster sauce
1 tablespoon patis (fish sauce)
¼ teaspoon achiote powder
7 ounces pancit canton (Chinese-style wheat noodles)
9 ounces pancit bihon (rice noodles)
Salt and white pepper to taste

For the garnish:
2 each hard-boiled eggs, cut into quarters
2 tablespoon finely sliced green onion
2 each calamansi, cut into wedges OR limes

Pancit is the Filipino term for noodles, so I suppose this dish is called "noodles noodles." Of the many kinds of noodles made and sold in the Philippines, this dish uses two, pancit canton and pancit bihon. You'll probably find them in the Asian section of your supermarket. If necessary, you can substitute Chinese wheat noodles and rice sticks.

Achiote powder and achiote oil are used in many Latin American dishes. They are made from annatto seeds. If you can't find achiote powder in the store, look for achiote oil; if you can't find the oil, look for the seeds and make your own oil or use the one in the Community Recipes chapter. Don't try to grind the seeds yourself. They are very hard. Also, be careful not to spill powder or oil on any good clothing or kitchen towels; the seeds leave a permanent stain. This is the Pang 'ohana's recipe.

The shrimp are frozen and should be peeled and deveined.

Prepare the lup cheong, onions, celery, garlic, and carrots per the instructions in the ingredients list. Boil the eggs for the garnish; cool under cold running water so that they will be easy to peel. Peel and cut into quarters. Cut up the green onion and calamansi per the instructions in the ingredients list.

Heat oil in a wok. Add the Chinese sausage, garlic, and onions and stir-fry. Next add the shrimp and vegetables. Add in the broth, oyster sauce, patis, achiote powder, and the noodles. Continue cooking until the noodles have absorbed the stock and are soft and pliable. Season with salt and pepper.

PRESENTATION

Divide the pancit among 4 bowls. Add a quartered hard-boiled egg and chopped green onions to each bowl and serve the calamansi wedges on the side. Serve immediately.

Plantation-Inspired Cuisine

Miso Soup with Anuhea Farms Asparagus

The sweetness of this Maui-grown asparagus is the star in this very humble miso soup dish. It is quick and easy to prepare and makes a great beginning for any meal.

Trim the tough ends from the asparagus. You can do this by experimentally bending the stem, starting at the head and moving down the stem, until you reach a portion of stalk that doesn't want to bend. That is the tough part. Snap it off.

Heat a large pot of water over medium-high heat. When it is boiling, add the asparagus spears. Cook them for approximately 3 to 5 minutes, or until they turn a bright green. Thin stalks will cook in 3 minutes, thick ones may take closer to 5.

Do not overcook the asparagus. The minute that it's done, remove it from the water and plunge it into a bowl of ice water. This stops the cooking and keeps the asparagus fresh and crisp.

When the asparagus has cooled, drain it and cut it into 1½-inch long pieces on the diagonal. Cut the tofu into 1-inch cubes. Finely slice the green onions.

Measure 6 cups of water into a large pot and bring it to a boil. Lower the heat and add the hondashi. Whisk in the two types of miso paste. Warm up the soup but do not let it boil.

PRESENTATION

Divide the cut-up tofu and asparagus evenly among 8 soup bowls. Ladle soup into each bowl. Garnish with the sliced green onions.

Yield: 6 to 8 servings

16 stalks of asparagus
10 ounces (½ of a 20-ounce block) firm tofu
¼ cup finely sliced green onion
6 cups water
2 teaspoons hondashi
4 tablespoons aka miso
2 tablespoons white miso

Lobster Tempura

Yield: 4 servings

8 (3- to 4-ounce) Tristan
lobster tails, frozen
Oil for deep-frying

For the batter:
¾ cup all-purpose flour
½ cup cornstarch
½ tablespoon baking powder
¼ teaspoon salt
1 cup ice-cold water (adjust
water if thinner batter
desired)

*For the grapefruit soy
sauce:*
2 tablespoons soy sauce
1 tablespoon grapefruit
juice

For the chili aioli sauce:
2 tablespoons mayonnaise
½ teaspoon sambal oelek
(Indonesian chili paste)

*For the pineapple sweet
chili sauce:*
2 tablespoons sweet Thai
chili sauce
1 tablespoon minced fresh
pineapple

For the garnish (optional):
24 steamed asparagus
spears

*S*weet cold-water lobster tails make this lobster tempura dish special. I prefer Tristan lobster tails. Their shells are thin and the meat is exceptionally sweet. You can find these tails at The Seafood Connection. They are harvested in Tristan, the most remote inhabited (barely) island in the world, located in the middle of the Atlantic ocean. Its rock lobster fishery practices sustainable aquaculture, for which it has received many awards.

Mix up all the dipping sauces. They are all very easy. All you need to do is measure the ingredients into three small bowls and mix. If you think your family or guests might want more sauce, you can double or triple the quantities.

Defrost the lobster tails in the refrigerator for best results.

Split the lobster tails in half lengthwise. Gently pull lobster meat from shell, leaving the meat attached to the tail end of the shell.

Put all the dry ingredients (flour, cornstarch, baking powder, and salt) for the batter in a bowl and whisk them together. Gradually add the water, whisking the batter as you pour. Don't feel that you need to add all the water; if the batter looks fine to you, stop pouring. Try not to over-mix the batter. That would release the gluten in the flour and make the tempura coating tough and chewy.

Heat the oil in your deep-fryer or deep saucepot to 350 degrees (a frying thermometer would help). Hold a lobster tail by the shell and dip the dangling tail meat into the batter and then into the hot oil. Fry the lobster until it is crisp, or about 1½ to 2 minutes. Drain on paper towels. Repeat until all the lobster tails are cooked.

We like to leave the tails on, as they turn red when cooked and make a great presentation.

PRESENTATION

Serve the lobster with the three dipping sauces on the side. Each tail can be garnished with 3 asparagus spears.

Portuguese Sweet Bread

Yield: 7 rolls per pan

½ cup warm but not hot
  water
1¼ cups evaporated milk
2¼ teaspoons (1 package)
  dry yeast
4 tablespoons butter,
  melted
1 large egg, beaten
½ cup sugar
1½ teaspoons salt
4 cups all-purpose flour

For the egg wash:
1 egg
2 tablespoons milk

If you have a stand mixer with a dough hook, you will find this bread easy to make. Most of the work consists of waiting for the dough to rise.

Experienced bakers will tell you to let the rolls cool before breaking them open, buttering, and eating them. The bread continues cooking, with residual heat, even after you take it out of the oven. If you eat the bread straight out of the oven, it may still be a little gummy in the center. However, even experienced bakers have difficulty restraining themselves when the bread smells and tastes SO GOOD!

Mix the water, evaporated milk, and yeast in the bowl of your stand mixer. You can use the paddle attachment for this first step. (If you don't have a mixer, beat well with a spoon.)

Melt the butter and beat the egg. Switch to the dough hook attachment for the mixer. Add the melted butter, egg, sugar, salt, and flour to the yeast and mix to combine.

Knead the dough with the dough hook until the dough is evenly mixed, soft, and pliable (or knead by hand if you don't have a stand mixer with a dough hook). The kneading may take 5 or 6 minutes with a mixer, as long as 10 by hand. The dough should collect in a lump while you are kneading it. If the dough is too sticky and clings to the sides of the bowl, add a little extra flour.

Lift the dough out of the mixing bowl, pour a little cooking oil into the bowl, and roll the ball of dough around in the oil. It should not stick to the walls of the bowl. It is OK if there are still some streaks of dried dough on the sides of the bowl; you can wash those out later.

Cover the bowl with a lid, a cloth, or a piece of plastic wrap. Put the bowl in a warm place, and let the dough rise until doubled. This will usually take about 1 hour, but if your kitchen is chilly, this may take longer.

Roll the dough into a long snake and divide it into 7 equal pieces. Roll the pieces into balls.

Oil a 10-inch diameter round pan. Arrange 6 of the dough balls around the edge of the pan and put 1 in the center. Cover the pan and let the dough rise again. It should rise for about 1 hour, or until the dough still bounces back when poked lightly with a finger. (If it doesn't bounce back, it is over-risen and won't have much oven spring.)

Before the dough has finished rising, preheat the oven to 350 degrees.

Beat the egg for the egg wash and mix it with the milk. Gently brush the egg wash over the top of the rolls. Careful; you don't want to deflate the rolls. Bake at 350 degrees for 30 to 40 minutes. Turn the rolls out of the pan and cool them on a wire rack.

Holy Ghost Church

When the parishioners of Kula's Holy Ghost Church were told that their hundred-year-old building had been infested by termites and needed to be torn down or rebuilt, they did not worry; they baked. Every weekend for a decade, they baked soft, delicious Portuguese sweet bread rolls and raised the $1 million they needed to rebuild the famous octagonal church. The building and its museum-quality altars were restored to a condition befitting the church's place on the state and national registers of historic places. And even though they made the last loan payment more than ten years ago, the dedicated bakers continue to bake every other weekend—just to keep up with demand for their famous bread.

Left to right: Agnes Lopes, Irene Otto, Dorothy DePonte, Beth Daniels, Carol Cablay (green shirt), Harriet Tavares (pink sweater), Jeanette Vares, Barbara Nakanelua, Elizabeth Varano, Charles Lopes

Not shown here: Adeline Franco, Betty Texeira, Agnes Lopes (there is two Agnes Lopes), Gertrude Aguirre, Patricia Fernandez, Eleanor Martin, Colleen Weimer, Nancy Purdy, Rosaline De Ponte

Korean-Style Spicy Chicken

This recipe for Korean-style spicy chicken is in the top five favorites at Kō, The Fairmont Kea Lani's signature restaurant. The chicken is marinated, served crisped with special sauce and drizzled with Ali'i Kula Lavender Farm Honey.

Mix marinade ingredients in a bowl. Cut the boneless chicken into 1½-inch chunks and place in the marinade. Marinate in refrigerator for at least 30 minutes.

Measure the cornstarch into a bowl or shallow-sided pan. Cover a baking sheet with plastic wrap. Drain the chicken chunks and dredge each piece in the cornstarch; lay the cornstarch-coated chicken pieces on the baking sheet and refrigerate for 20 minutes.

While the chicken is chilling, mix the dipping sauce. Peel and mince the garlic; peel and grate the ginger. Mix all sauce ingredients in a small bowl and set aside.

When the chicken has finished chilling, heat the oil in your deep-fryer or saucepot to 350 degrees (a frying thermometer will help you keep the oil at the proper temperature). Slip the chicken chunks into the hot oil and fry for 3 to 4 minutes, or until brown and crisp. Turn as necessary. You will probably need to do this in several batches; do not overcrowd the oil. Drain the fried chicken on paper towels to remove excess oil.

PRESENTATION

I like to dip all the chicken pieces in the sauce and drizzle them with honey. Sprinkles of toasted sesame seeds and finely sliced green onion complete the dish.

However, it's up to you if you'd like to just put out the dipping sauce and the garnishes next to a platter of fried chicken and let your family or guests season their own chicken.

Yield: 4 to 6 servings

1 pound boneless, skinless chicken thighs
1 cup cornstarch, for dredging
Oil, for deep-frying

For the marinade:
2 teaspoons sugar
1 tablespoon soy sauce
2 teaspoons rice wine
1 teaspoon sesame oil
1 teaspoon salt

For the dipping sauce:
1 teaspoon minced garlic
½ teaspoon peeled and grated ginger
4 tablespoons brown sugar
4 tablespoons soy sauce
2 tablespoons mirin
1 teaspoon sesame oil
¼ teaspoon dried chili flakes
2 tablespoons water

For the garnish:
Lavender honey (or honey of your choice)
Toasted sesame seeds
finely chopped green onion

Chicken and Shiitake Mushroom Lumpia

Yield: 4 servings
(16 lumpia)

16 lumpia wrappers (I like
the Menlo brand)

For the filling:
4 fresh shiitake mushrooms,
finely minced
3 tablespoons finely minced
Kula onion
3 tablespoons finely minced
carrot
2 tablespoons finely minced
celery
1 large egg, beaten
1 pound ground chicken
1 tablespoon soy sauce
1 teaspoon sesame oil
1 teaspoon salt
½ teaspoon ground pepper

*For the achara (green
papaya relish):*
1 large green papaya
1 small carrot, peeled and
julienned
¼ of a medium-sized red
bell pepper, julienned
2 tablespoons golden raisins
1 cup vinegar
1 cup brown sugar
1 teaspoon salt

*For the chili cilantro garlic
sauce:*
1 tablespoon chopped
cilantro
1 cup rice vinegar
⅔ cup Thai sweet chili sauce
1 teaspoon salt

*T*hese chicken lumpia are served with two tasty condiments. One of them, the achara (green papaya relish), has to be made the day before you plan to serve the lumpia. This relish will keep in the refrigerator for a couple of weeks, and the flavor gets better as it sits. It goes well with lumpia, shanghai or hot steamed rice. If you like it, make up a large batch and keep it on hand. It's a Filipino favorite, with many variations. The lumpia can be made ahead of time too; wrap and fill them, then freeze them before deep-frying them. Let them thaw before frying.

You will have to make the achara the day before you plan to serve the lumpia. Start by peeling and seeding the papaya. Cut the flesh into slices and then into julienne strips, about 1½ inches long and ⅛ inch wide. Peel and julienne the carrot; trim, de-seed, and julienne the red bell pepper. Do your best to make all the julienne strips the same size. Mix all the julienne strips with the raisins, vinegar, and brown sugar; cover the bowl, and let the relish marinate in the refrigerator overnight.

For the chili cilantro garlic sauce, wash, trim, and chop the cilantro. Combine vinegar and Thai sweet chili sauce in a small saucepan. Bring the mixture to a boil over medium-high heat. Remove from the heat, mix in the salt, and allow the sauce to cool. When it has cooled, add the chopped cilantro.

Wash the mushrooms; peel the onion and carrot; trim the celery. Mince fine; measure out the needed quantities and put them into a medium-sized bowl.

Beat the egg and add it to the bowl. Add the ground chicken, soy sauce, sesame oil, salt, and pepper. Mix the lumpia filling thoroughly.

Pull 16 lumpia wrappers off the stack of lumpia sheets and lay them out on a clean table or counter. The wrappers should be placed so that one point is facing you; they should look like diamonds, not squares. Set a small bowl of cold water off to one side.

Divide the filling evenly between the 16 wrappers. You may want to use your clean hands to form a ball of filling, then shape it into a roll. Place the roll about 2 inches above the lowest point of the wrapper, going across the wrapper.

(recipe continued on page 14)

Plantation-Inspired Cuisine

When the filling is divided, start rolling up the lumpia. Fold up the bottom part of the wrapper, over the filling, and start to roll. When you're halfway up, fold the wrapper points sticking out to the side into the roll. Keep rolling. Put a dab of water on the topmost wrapper point and use the moisture to seal the lumpia shut. Repeat until all the lumpia are rolled.

Heat the oil in your deep-fryer or a deep saucepot to 350 degrees (a deep-frying thermometer will help you keep an even temperature). Deep-fry the lumpia, turning as necessary, until they are crisp and golden brown. You will have to fry the lumpia in several batches. Do not crowd the oil; this lowers the oil temperature and makes the lumpia soggy and greasy. Drain the finished lumpia on paper towels.

Serve with chili cilantro garlic sauce and achara.

Plantation-Inspired Cuisine

Chop Chop Chicken Salad

It's a nice touch to chill the platter on which you'll serve the salad to help keep the salad crisp. This is your classic Chinese chicken salad using local produce. The name "Chop Chop" refers to the quickness with which everything can be made. It's comfort food with traditional flavors.

Cook the chicken breasts. Whether you're grilling or broiling, the breasts will stay moist and juicy if you brine them before cooking them. Mix the salt, sugar, and water in a large zip-lock plastic bag and add the chicken breasts. Press out as much air as you can and seal the bag. Refrigerate the breasts for one hour. Remove them from the brine, rinse and dry. Grill or broil.

Cut the cooked and cooled breasts across the grain, into strips 1½ inches long and about ⅛-inch wide.

Put the serving platter in the refrigerator to chill (optional).

Trim and shred the lettuce and cabbage. The shreds should be about ¼ inch wide. Trim and deseed the bell pepper; cut it into julienne strips about 1½ inches long and ⅛ inch wide. Peel and trim the carrots, cut into 1⅓ inch long slices, and then cut the slices into ⅛-inch julienne strips.

Whisk together all the ingredients for the salad dressing. The oil should be completely emulsified, not floating in globules.

Slice the won ton wrappers into ¼-inch-wide strips. Heat the oil in a deep-fryer or a deep saucepot to 350 degrees. Fry the strips until brown and crispy. You will probably have to do this in several batches; don't crowd the oil. Remove the cooked strips and let them drain on paper towels.

Wash and trim the cilantro for the garnish.

Mix the shredded lettuce and won bok and the julienned bell pepper and carrots in a large salad bowl. Add the sliced chicken and mix again. Pour ¼ cup of the salad dressing over the salad and toss.

PRESENTATION

Transfer the salad to a chilled serving platter. Garnish the salad with the crisp won ton strips and cilantro sprigs.

Yield: 4 servings

8 ounces (½-pound) chicken breast
2 cups shredded iceberg lettuce
2 cups shredded won bok cabbage
¼ cup julienned red bell pepper
¼ cup julienned carrot

For the brine:
2 tablespoons Hawaiian or kosher salt
2 tablespoons sugar
1 cup water

For the dressing:
¼ cup rice vinegar
⅓ cup vegetable oil
1½ tablespoons sesame oil
3 tablespoons sugar
¾ teaspoon freshly ground black pepper
½ tablespoon salt

For the garnish:
8 won ton wrappers, cut into thin strips and deep-fried OR won ton pi chips from the supermarket
8 sprigs cilantro

Kobe Beef Poke

*T*he original Japanese Kobe beef comes from Hyōgo Prefecture in Japan, where Wagyu cattle are pampered with prime feed and massage. Their meat is tender, well-marbled, and flavorful. Kobe beef is extremely expensive in Japan, and even more expensive when exported overseas. American ranchers saw opportunity here and developed American-grown Kobe-style beef, from Wagyu-Angus crossbred cattle given much the same treatment as Japan's pampered Kobe cattle. American Kobe-style beef is very good, and less expensive than Japanese Kobe beef. The Maui Prime gourmet grocery in Lahaina stocks this Kobe-style beef, which is becoming increasingly popular with high-end restaurants and discerning home cooks.

Sambal oelek is an Indonesian chili paste. You can find it at most grocery stores on Maui. You can also substitute Vietnamese chili paste or Korean chili paste.

To make the steak rub, mince the garlic, chop the parsley, and combine with the chili flakes, salt, and sugar.

To make the relish, cut up the onion, tomato, and cucumber per the instructions in the ingredients list. Combine the chopped veggies with the sesame oil and chili paste.

Massage the rub into both sides of the steaks. Heat up your grill. When the grill is hot, sear the steaks. They should be cooked on the outside and rare or medium-rare in the center. Let steaks rest for 10 minutes.

Cut the seared steaks into 1-inch cubes. Put the cubes into a serving bowl, add the relish, and toss. Serve immediately.

Yield: 4 to 6 servings

4 (4-ounce) Kobe-style beef flat-iron steaks

For the steak rub:
½ tablespoon minced garlic
½ tablespoon chopped parsley
¾ teaspoon dried chili flakes
2 tablespoons Hawaiian 'alaea salt
2 tablespoons turbinado sugar (Maui raw sugar)

For the relish:
¼ cup diced Kula onion (¼-inch dice)
¼ cup diced tomato (¼-inch dice)
¼ cup diced Japanese cucumber (¼-inch dice)
1½ tablespoons sesame oil
1 teaspoon sambal oelek (Indonesian chili paste)

Taste of Tofu

Yield: 3 to 4 servings

20 ounces (1 block) tofu
¼ cup flour (optional)
3 heads of assorted baby
   lettuce or 2 cups of
   washed and cut greens
Oil for deep-frying
   (optional)

For the garnishes:
¼ cup chopped sea
   asparagus (about 1 ounce)
¼ cup cherry tomatoes,
   cut in half
4 sprigs cilantro

For the dressing:
2 teaspoons finely sliced
   green onions
⅓ teaspoon finely grated
   ginger
¼ teaspoon chili pepper
   flakes
2 tablespoons oyster sauce
1 tablespoon soy sauce
1 teaspoon sugar
1 teaspoon sesame oil

This salad features locally made tofu (many brands available) and locally grown sea asparagus. Sea asparagus, also known as pickleweed and marsh samphire, grows in seashore marshes. Here in the Islands, it's grown on rafts in Kahuku, O'ahu, seashore ponds. It's crisp, salty, and a refreshing touch in stir-fries and salads. It's showing up in many high-end restaurants. You can buy the sea asparagus at Kula Produce Company on Maui.

Just about everyone loves the crunch of deep-fried tofu, but some of us have to watch our waistlines. We enjoy our tofu in its natural state. The flavor is subtler but still very pleasant. Feel free to skip the deep-frying and serve a lighter, leaner salad.

Cut tofu into 1-inch cubes. Wash and cut up or tear the greens.

Fill a medium-sized pot with water and bring to a boil. Add the sea asparagus and blanch for approximately 30 seconds. Remove it from the boiling water and submerge it in a bowl of ice water, to stop the cooking.

Prepare the salad dressing: slice the green onions, and peel and grate the ginger. Put the green onions, ginger, chili flakes, oyster sauce, soy sauce, sugar, and sesame oil in a bowl and whisk together until the oil is emulsified.

If you are going to serve the tofu deep-fried, dredge the cubes in the flour. Heat the oil in a deep-fryer or deep saucepot to 350 degrees (use a deep-frying thermometer if you don't have a deep-fryer with a built-in thermometer). Slip the cubes into the hot oil and fry, turning as necessary, until crisp and golden brown. You will probably have to do this in several batches, so that you don't crowd the oil. Put the fried cubes on paper towels to drain.

PRESENTATION

Arrange the greens on a serving platter and top with tofu cubes, fried or raw. Drizzle the dressing over the salad. Top with the sea asparagus, tomato, and cilantro garnishes.

Oishii Sushi

*O*ishii sushi literally translates to "Good Sushi," which is the comment we get from guests who have enjoyed this dish. It is a non-traditional spicy tuna roll that is lightly cooked tempura-style.

Make the sushi vinegar by placing all ingredients in a small saucepan and heating over low heat until the sugar has completely dissolved. Remove the piece of kombu.

Cook short-grain rice in your rice cooker and measure out 2 cups cooked rice. Put the rice into a sushi bucket, if you have one, or a shallow baking dish. Pour a little of the sushi vinegar over the rice and turn the rice with a wooden spoon or spatula. Keep pouring sushi-zu and turning the rice. As the rice cools, it will absorb the vinegar. Speed the cooling by fanning the rice while turning it. Old-fashioned cooks used a hand fan; modern cooks put an electric table fan next to the rice.

Mince the 'ahi and mix it with the sesame oil and salt.

Prepare the tempura batter by whisking together the flour, cornstarch, baking powder, and salt. Slowly add the ice water, whisking as you go. You do not need to add all the water; stop when the batter seems right to you. It should be neither stiff nor runny; it should be thick enough to coat a spoon. Try not to over-mix, as this will develop the gluten and make the tempura tough.

Prepare the garnishes per the directions in the ingredients list.

Put the sheets of nori on a clean counter or table, shiny side down. Divide the sushi rice into 4 equal portions (if you've used a baking pan to make the sushi rice, you can pat the rice flat and use a wooden spatula to cut it into 4 sections). Put a portion of rice on each piece of nori. Spread it evenly over the bottom ¾ of each sheet. Spoon ¼ of the seasoned 'ahi into each sheet of nori and rice. The 'ahi mixture should form a horizontal line in the middle of the rice. Starting with the end nearest you, start rolling up the nori and rice. Try to keep the roll nice and tight. You will end with the nori that isn't covered with rice; smooth this over the roll, to close the roll.

(recipe continued on page 22)

Yield: 4 servings

- 2 cups cooked short-grain rice
- ½ cup sushi vinegar (sushi-zu) (see recipe below)
- 1 pound sashimi-grade 'ahi
- 2 tablespoons sesame oil
- 1½ teaspoons Hawaiian 'alaea salt
- 4 sheets yaki nori (crisp squares of seaweed)
- 2 cups tempura batter (see recipe below)
- Oil for deep frying

For the sushi vinegar (sushi-zu):
- ½ cup rice vinegar
- ½ cup sugar
- 2 tablespoons mirin
- 1 teaspoon salt
- 1 (2-inch by 3-inch) piece dried kombu seaweed

For the tempura batter:
- 1½ cups all-purpose flour
- 1 cup cornstarch
- 1 tablespoon baking powder
- ½ teaspoon salt
- 2 cups ice water

(ingredients continued on page 22)

For the garnish:

- 1 tablespoon orange tobiko caviar
- ¼ cup kaiware (radish) sprouts, bottom inch of roots cut off
- 1 tablespoon Chili Aioli (see page 6)
- 1 tablespoon Kabayaki sauce (Kosso Brand, available in the Asian section at most grocery stores)

Put the roll on a sudare, a bamboo sushi mat. Roll up the mat, using it to firm and shape the roll.

Heat the oil in a deep-fryer or a deep saucepot to 350 degrees. If you don't have a deep-fryer with a built-in thermometer, it's a good idea to use a frying thermometer. Dip a finished roll into the tempura batter and slide it into the hot oil. Fry it for 30 seconds or until crisp. Remove the roll from the oil and drain it on paper towels. Repeat until all the rolls are fried.

PRESENTATION

Slice each roll into 8 slices, using a sharp knife that is cleaned with a damp cloth between each cut. Arrange the deep-fried sushi on a serving platter or on individual plates. Garnish the sushi with orange tobiko and kaiware sprouts. Serve with Chili Aioli and Kabayaki sauce drizzled over the sliced sushi roll.

Shrimp and Lup Cheong Fried Rice

I'm not going to tell you to cook rice for this recipe because it starts with leftover rice, rice that's been left to cool. Fried rice made with fresh rice just doesn't taste the same. Fried rice from Chinese home kitchens is always different. It's usually made from leftovers (leftover rice, leftover meat, leftover veggies) fried together. You can also kick it up with shrimp or lobster. It's a great meal, any time of day.

This fried rice is humble but tasty. You can use peeled and deveined fresh shrimp (or frozen shrimp that has already been peeled and deveined) and frozen pea and carrot mix. You probably have some lup cheong, green onions, and eggs in the refrigerator. When you need something that you can cook in a hurry, without a trip to the store, this is it.

Thaw the frozen shrimp and the peas and carrots mix. If you're in a hurry, run them under cold water to thaw them fast. Drain well. Cut the shrimp in half lengthwise. Dice the lup cheong and slice the green onions. Beat the eggs in a small bowl.

Heat 1 tablespoon of the oil in a wok over medium heat. Add the beaten eggs and swirl them around the pan. Flip with your wok spatula to cook both sides. When the eggs are cooked, remove them from the wok and set them aside on a plate. Cut into ½-inch bits.

Add the remaining 1 tablespoon of vegetable oil to the wok. Add the sesame oil as well. When the oil is hot and fragrant, put the shrimp in the wok and stir-fry for 30 seconds. Add the diced lup cheong bits and the peas and carrots, and continue stir-frying. When they have warmed up, add the leftover rice. Stir-fry until the rice has warmed and softened a little. Add the oyster sauce, soy sauce, salt and pepper and mix well. Add the cooked egg, the chopped green onions, and mix again. Season with salt and pepper, remove from the heat and serve immediately.

Yield: 4 servings

- 4 (13/15 size) raw peeled and deveined shrimp, thawed and sliced in half lengthwise
- ¼ cup thawed peas and carrots mix
- 1 (approximately 4-inch) stick of lup cheong (Chinese sausage), cut into ¼-inch dice
- ¼ cup sliced green onions
- 2 whole eggs, beaten
- 1 + 1 tablespoons vegetable oil
- 1 teaspoon sesame oil
- 2½ cups cooked jasmine rice
- 1 tablespoon oyster sauce
- 1 teaspoon soy sauce
- Salt and pepper to taste

Grilled Miso Shrimp with Soba Noodles

This recipe is a combination of two favorite dishes: grilled miso shrimp and chilled buckwheat soba noodles. It is a great summer dish that I like to serve with baby lettuce leaves, to be eaten like a lettuce wrap. The melding of these simple flavors tests the palate. Crunchy sweet shrimp with smooth mildly salty noodles in a healthy refreshing lettuce wrap.

Put the dried wakame in a small bowl and add warm water to cover. Soak it for 15 minutes; drain.

Bring a large pot of water to boil and add the dry soba. Cook until the noodles have softened, about 4 minutes, and test the noodles before draining into a colander. Run cold water over them to stop the cooking.

Prepare the sauce by mixing the water, shiki no irodori, mirin, and soy sauce in a small saucepot and bringing the mixture to a boil. Remove the sauce from the heat and allow it to cool.

Mix the cooked and drained soba, the drained wakame, and the cooled sauce.

Peel and devein the shrimp. Whisk marinade ingredients together in a bowl. Add the shrimp and marinate for 20 minutes.

While the shrimp is marinating, wash and drain the green leaf lettuce. Slice the green onions and bell pepper per the ingredients list.

Heat a charcoal or gas grill. Grill the shrimp over moderate heat, for 1 minute on each side. Remove the cooked shrimp to a plate.

PRESENTATION

Arrange the seasoned soba noodles on a serving platter and top with the grilled miso shrimp. Garnish the shrimp with the green onions and peppers and serve with the green leaf lettuce.

Yield: 4 servings

1 pound soba (buckwheat noodles)
1 tablespoon dried wakame
20 (13/15 size) raw shrimp, peeled and deveined
20 leaves of green leaf lettuce
2 tablespoons finely sliced green onions
¼ red bell pepper cut julienned

For the shrimp marinade:
1 tablespoon aka miso
1 tablespoon tahini
1 tablespoon sesame oil
1 tablespoon soy sauce
1 tablespoon honey
¼ cup orange juice

For the soba noodle sauce:
1 cup water
¼ cup shiki no irodori soup stock (Hichifuku brand)
¼ cup mirin
1½ tablespoons soy sauce

House Cake Noodles

Yield: 4 servings

¼ cup thin-sliced onions

4 shiitake mushrooms, quartered

¼ cup sliced carrots (⅛-inch round slices)

¼ cup sliced zucchini (¼-inch round slices)

1 cup of baby bok choy, cut into 1-inch pieces

¼ cups red bell pepper, diced 1 inch (about ¼ of a medium-sized bell pepper)

8 ounces fresh saimin noodles

8 (13/15 size) raw shrimp, peeled and deveined

2 + 2 tablespoons vegetable oil

2 cups chicken stock

2 tablespoons oyster sauce

2 tablespoons soy sauce

1 teaspoon sesame oil

1 teaspoon salt

½ teaspoon pepper

For the cornstarch slurry:

1½ tablespoons cornstarch

½ cup water

This is my dad, Yun Young Pang's, recipe. I remember as if it were yesterday, standing beside him in our small kitchen trying to figure out the ingredients to our favorite restaurant dish. Many trials and errors produced these amazing flavors. Dad finally figured it out. Every holiday, get together, any party, this is the dish most requested from our family kitchen.

Cut up the onions, mushrooms, carrots, zuchinni, bok choy, and red bell pepper per the instructions in the ingredients list.

Fill a large pot with water and bring to a boil. Add the saimin noodles and cook noodles for 2 minutes. Remove from water, drain in colander, rinse with cold water, drain again.

Prepare the shrimp by peeling them and removing the veins.

Heat the 2 tablespoons of oil in a wok over medium-high heat. When the oil is hot, add the noodles. Spread them over the bottom of the wok so that they form a cake or pancake. Cook them until the cake is crisp and brown on one side. Flip it over and crisp the other side. You may need to add a little more oil to keep the cake from sticking. When the cake is cooked, remove it to a serving platter and cut it into 4 or more pieces.

Add the other 2 tablespoons of oil to the wok. Stir-fry the shrimp and chopped vegetables; this may take 3 to 4 minutes.

Add the chicken stock, oyster sauce, soy sauce, sesame oil, salt, and pepper to the wok and stir to mix. Bring the contents of the wok to a boil, then lower the heat. Mix the cornstarch and cold water into a slurry, and stir the slurry into the mixture in the wok. Keep stirring as the sauce thickens.

PRESENTATION

Pour the contents of the wok over the cut-up noodle cake and serve immediately.

Grown on Maui

BUY LOCAL...sustainably grown ingredients! It's the right thing to do, for the environment and for the local economy. Shortening the distance between farm and table—sometimes to only a few miles—not only supports our local, multi-generational farming families, it also reduces the financial and environmental costs of shipping food in from the mainland. But those aren't the only reasons we do it. We also buy local because it just tastes better. There's just no comparison between a tomato that's been grown on the mainland and shipped while it's still hard and green, and a tomato grown in the rich volcanic soil of Kula, irrigated by sustainable rain-catchment systems, allowed to ripen on the vine, and harvested a day or two before we serve it in a salad.

In addition to local produce, buy local meat, dairy, poultry, and eggs. Please try some of the 'ono recipes in this chapter, using ingredients from suppliers like Haleakalā Ranch, Surfing Goat Dairy, Neighborhood Farm Organic Eggs and Hana Fresh Farms. Be sure to check out your local farmers' market, too. It's another wonderful way to get the absolute freshest produce, and support your organic backyard farmers at the same time. It's thanks to these dedicated individuals that my colleagues and I can take Maui cooking to the next level.

Maui Cattle Company Paniolo Rib-Eye Steak

Yield: 4 to 5 servings

2 each (16- to 18- ounce)
Maui Cattle Company
bone-in rib-eye steaks

For the steak rub:
1 teaspoon chopped garlic
1 teaspoon chopped parsley
½ teaspoon dried chili
pepper flakes
2 tablespoons turbinado
sugar (Maui raw sugar)
2 tablespoons Hawaiian
'alaea salt

*M*aui Cattle Company was formed in 2002, by a group of independent ranchers who wanted to market their free-range, naturally raised, local meat under a recognizable brand name. Local chefs immediately recognized the quality of their offerings, and their flavorful beef is now featured on the menus of many Maui fine restaurants. When you buy this great meat, you aren't just buying tasty, healthy, local meat; you're also supporting Maui's century-old paniolo heritage and its independent ranchers.

Chop the garlic and parsley. Mix all ingredients for the rub and apply it to the steaks.

Grill steaks about 4 to 5 minutes on each side (or to your taste). You'll get the best flavor if you grill over a kiawe wood fire.

PRESENTATION

Let the steak rest for a few minutes before serving.

Coconut-Curry Haleakalā Ranch Lamb Chops with Mango Salsa

Maui Cattle Company's Haleakalā Ranch lamb comes from herds raised on the slopes of our majestic volcano. These free-range, grass-fed animals can be seen grazing as you drive the Upcountry roads. The meat is tender and flavorful. It's sold in a few Upcountry and Kula markets. Do look for it; it's a must-try for lamb lovers.

Mix all the marinade ingredients in a bowl. Place the lamb chops in the marinade. Coat well, cover, and refrigerate for 4 hours. Turn after two hours so the lamb can marinate evenly.

Make the fresh salsa while the lamb is marinating. Prepare the mango, red onion, bell pepper, mint, and lime juice according to the ingredient list. Mix all ingredients in a small bowl, cover, and set aside.

Grill the marinated lamb over medium heat. If you are using kiawe charcoal, make sure the coals are covered with a coating of light ash once the fire has died down. This will allow the lamb to cook without burning and will give the lamb a nice smoky taste when grilled. I like my chops 3 to 4 minutes on each side, but you can cook them to your own taste.

PRESENTATION

Remove the lamb chops from the grill, plate, and serve topped with the fresh mango salsa.

Yield: 4 servings

2 racks of lamb, cut into double-bone chops

For the marinade:
½ cup soy sauce
1 cup coconut cream (top 8-ounce portion of the can of coconut milk)
3 tablespoons curry powder
2 tablespoons minced garlic
1 tablespoon brown cane sugar

For the salsa:
2 cups diced mango
¼ cup diced red onion (¼-inch dice)
¼ cup diced bell pepper (¼-inch dice)
4 sprigs mint leaves (discard stems), chopped
2 tablespoons fresh lime juice (juice of 1 average lime)
¼ cup olive oil
Salt and pepper to taste

Surfing Goat Dairy Cheese Flat Bread with Caramelized Kula Onions

Yield: 4 servings

1 pound pizza dough
   OR 4 naan or pita breads
2 large Kula onions, thinly
   sliced
4 ounces Surfing Goat Dairy
   feta cheese, chopped or
   crumbled
8 large basil leaves, sliced
   thin or cut chiffonade
1 + 1 tablespoon olive oil
1 teaspoon sea salt or
   Hawaiian salt
½ teaspoon freshly ground
   pepper

Maui's Surfing Goat Dairy, located in Kula, has been producing gourmet cheeses for over nine years. Not only do owners Thomas and Eva Kafsack make great cheese, they've turned their company into a tourist attraction: the dairy offers guided tours of their operations. You can even milk a goat and help make cheese!

The recipe calls for pizza dough. We haven't included a recipe for making the dough, assuming that if you're comfortable baking your own bread and making your own pizza dough, you already have a favorite recipe for pizza crust. If you're not a bread baker, you can buy balls of refrigerated or frozen dough at the market. If you can't find the frozen dough, you can also use naan or pita as a base for the cheese and onions.

If your pizza dough is refrigerated, you're going to want to let it sit on the counter for an hour or so, until it reaches room temperature.

Divide the pizza dough into 4 even portions; pat and stretch each ball of dough into a circle. Put the 4 circles of dough on a lightly greased baking sheet and set aside.

Cut up the onions; chop or crumble the cheese; slice the basil leaves into thin slivers. If you want to practice your knife skills, try stacking the basil leaves and then rolling them into a cylinder. Cut thin slices across the cylinder. This chiffonade cut quickly turns the basil into elegant, even strips.

Heat 1 tablespoon of the olive oil in a skillet over medium heat. Add the sliced onions and cook, stirring frequently, until caramelized. This may take 30 minutes or more. Watch the onions carefully; they must not burn. If they are starting to get too brown on the edges, lower the heat.

Preheat the oven to 425 degrees.

Brush the pizza dough with the rest of the olive oil and sprinkle with the sea salt. Spread an even layer of caramelized onions over each circle of dough, then another even layer of goat cheese.

Bake at 425 degrees for about 8 minutes, or until the dough is crisp. Sprinkle each round with the sliced basil and serve immediately.

Anuhea Farms Stir-Fried Asparagus and Scallops

*M*uch of the asparagus eaten in the Islands is grown in California's hot, flat central valley and shipped over here. Lucky we live Maui! We can buy fresh asparagus from Anuhea Farms. Bill Mertins is growing wonderful asparagus up in the clouds in Makawao, at the 2,500-foot level. His asparagus is harvested and delivered on the same day; it is truly fresh asparagus. If you are fortunate enough to visit Bill at the farm and he lets you enjoy a just-picked asparagus spear, consider yourself lucky. There's nothing comparable. Bill's asparagus is available almost all year round and can be found at select local and farmers' markets.

Snap off the tough ends of the asparagus. (If you bend the stalk, you'll find the point at which it refuses to bend; that's the woody part and that's where you'll snap it.) Cut the stalks into 1-inch pieces, slicing on the bias. This exposes more of the inner stalk. Mince the ginger and garlic.

Pour the chicken stock, soy sauce, and oyster sauce into a small bowl and mix well. Add the cornstarch and stir until there are no lumps.

Set a wok or a large frying pan over high heat and add a few teaspoons of oil. When the oil is hot, add the ginger, garlic, and red chili flakes. Cook and stir briefly, then add the cut asparagus and scallops. Stir-fry the mixture for 2 minutes. Stir in the stock and cornstarch. Keep stirring until the sauce thickens.

PRESENTATION

Serve with rice or over noodles.

Yield: 4 servings

1½ pounds asparagus (medium thickness)
1½ cups chicken stock
1 tablespoon soy sauce
1 tablespoon oyster sauce
1 tablespoon cornstarch
1 tablespoon peeled and minced ginger
2 medium cloves garlic, minced
¼ teaspoon red chili flakes
1 pound (20/30) scallops, rinsed
Oil for stir-frying

Kula Baby Greens and Pohole Fern Shoots with Passion Fruit-Vanilla Vinaigrette

Yield: 4 to 6 servings

¼ pound Kula baby greens or local lettuces
¼ pound pohole fern shoots
2 ounces hearts of palm, sliced in thin strips
¼ cup cherry tomatoes, cut in quarters
4 tablespoons finely chopped toasted macadamia nuts
Freshly ground pepper to taste

For the passion fruit-vanilla vinaigrette:

4 tablespoons passion-fruit purée
½ teaspoon pure vanilla extract
OR scrapings from ¼ of a vanilla bean
¼ cup sugar
2 tablespoons rice wine vinegar
1½ cups of a light blended olive oil
Salt to taste

Soft and tender baby greens make a wonderful salad. If your market doesn't stock baby greens, use the best local lettuce you can find. Most of the ingredients in this salad can be locally sourced—if not from Maui, then from one of the other islands. Hearts of palm, for instance, are grown on the Big Island, as are macadamia nuts. You'll be amazed at the difference it makes to buy locally. Flavors are so fresh and vivid!

The vinaigrette is made with passion fruit purée. You may find this in the market as unsweetened liliko'i concentrate. You can also make your own purée, from passion fruit flesh put through a sieve. Throw out (or plant) the seed and save the sieved pulp. If you like to cook with liliko'i, make a lot and freeze it in plastic bags.

Make the dressing first, as it should chill. Put the passion fruit purée, vanilla, sugar, and vinegar in a bowl and whisk until well-combined. Slowly add the oil, whisking well between each addition. Put the dressing in the refrigerator to chill.

It's an extra-nice touch to also chill the platter or plates on which you'll compose the salad.

To clean the greens or lettuces, remove the stems and rinse the lettuce in a cold water bath; drain well.

Cut the pohole fern shoots into 2-inch pieces and blanch in salted water for 30 seconds. Cool in an ice-water bath and drain.

Cut up the heart of palm, tomato, and macadamia nuts per the instructions in the ingredients list.

PRESENTATION

Arrange the baby greens on a chilled platter or individual plates and arrange the hearts of palm and tomato on top. Sprinkle the macadamia nuts over all. Drizzle the salad with the chilled dressing and add salt and pepper to taste.

Serve immediately.

Sweet Kula Corn Pudding

F resh corn is good, but the sugar starts to break down soon after it is harvested. Refrigeration slows down the process. Corn is high in fiber and carbohydrates, and low in sodium. The farmers deliver Maui Super Sweet Corn from Kula daily.

Emeril Lagasse presented a classic Southern-style corn pudding. My recipe uses fresh, plump Kula corn. We stepped up the presentation by lining the muffin tins with the corn husks to create a mini cupcake serving. This recipe is understated! Try it and you'll understand.

Yield: 6 servings

6 ears fresh Kula sweet corn (or the freshest corn you can buy)
2 tablespoons finely diced Kula onions (or local sweet onions)
½ cup grated Parmesan cheese
2 tablespoons butter
2 cups heavy cream
1 cup milk
6 whole eggs
½ cup corn meal
1 teaspoon salt
¼ teaspoon white pepper
⅛ teaspoon nutmeg

Preheat the oven to 350 degrees.

Shuck the corn, saving the husks. Using a coarse grater, grate the corn kernels off the cob and into a bowl. Dice the onions. Grate the Parmesan cheese if you aren't using commercial pre-grated cheese.

Heat the butter in a frying pan over medium heat. Sauté the onions in the butter until they have softened; add the grated corn and continue to sauté on moderate heat for another 3 minutes.

Put the cream, milk, eggs, and cheese in a mixing bowl and whisk together. Add this to the corn mixture, stirring constantly over low heat. Gradually add the corn meal, salt, pepper, and nutmeg, and continue cooking and stirring for another 1½ minutes.

Spray a 6-cup muffin tin with non-stick spray and line the cups with the saved corn husks. The husks make natural muffin cups. Divide the batter evenly between the cups. Bake at 350 degrees for approximately 20 minutes or until the tops are nicely browned and the centers of the muffins are no longer liquid. (Use a toothpick or paring knife to test.)

Sweet Kula Onion Soup

Yield: 6 servings

4 pounds sweet Kula onions
4 tablespoons butter
1 teaspoon salt
½ cup dry sherry
4 cups beef broth
4 cups chicken broth
4 fresh sprigs of thyme
1 bay leaf
12 slices (½-inch thick)
   from a long French
   baguette
6 (1-ounce) slices Gruyère
   cheese

The sweet Kula onions are the key ingredients to this delightful onion soup. The onions for this recipe come from Bryan Otani Farms in Upcountry Kula. If you have a chance to visit this wonderful family-run operation, you will find more than just onions. They have string beans, eggplant, red cabbage, and much more, depending on the season. Their sustainably grown produce can be found in select Maui markets.

Peel and slice the onions; slices should be approximately ¼-inch thick.

Heat the butter in a heavy-bottomed, 2-gallon soup pot set over medium heat. Add the onions and salt and sauté until the onions are soft and nicely caramelized. This will take at least 30 minutes; keep the heat moderate and stir periodically to keep the onions from burning. Don't rush this process.

Deglaze the pot with the sherry, and add the chicken and beef stock. Bring to a boil. Add the thyme and bay leaf (if you're going to remove them later, add them in a spice bag). Turn heat down and simmer on low for 30 minutes. Remove the herbs and season with salt and pepper.

Toast the sliced baguettes.

Preheat the oven to 400 degrees.

Divide the onion soup between 6 oven-proof soup bowls. Top each bowl with two slices of toasted baguette and a slice of Gruyère cheese. Bake in a 400 degree oven until the cheese is browned, or about 5 minutes. Check the soup occasionally to make sure that you don't burn the cheese.

Maui Cattle Company
Chinese Five-Spice Boneless Short Ribs

(Courtesy of Chef Becky Speere)

Yield: 4 servings

This recipe is wonderful made with just any short ribs, but it's better than wonderful when prepared with locally raised Maui Cattle Company beef. It's a Crock-Pot recipe that requires a ten-hour cooking time. Start it early in the morning for a delicious, no-fuss dinner. If you don't want to get up at the crack of dawn to make this for dinner, cook overnight, put in the refrigerator, and reheat. Stews often improve when they are allowed to sit before being reheated.

Approximately 2 to 3 pieces of boneless short ribs would be the equivalent of 4 pounds. Prepare the green onions, garlic, and ginger per the instructions in the ingredients list.

Lightly flour the short ribs. Heat the 2 tablespoons of oil in a large frying pan over medium-high heat; brown the ribs.

Put the short ribs in a Crock-Pot. Add the rest of the recipe ingredients, including the prepared onion, garlic, and ginger. Mix well. Cook for 10 hours on the Crock-Pot's medium setting.

PRESENTATION

Chef Becky Speere likes to serve these ribs over hot rice, with Maui-grown pickled vegetables on the side.

4 pounds short ribs
1 cup sliced green onion (½-inch slices)
3 medium cloves garlic, thinly sliced
2 tablespoons ginger, peeled and thinly sliced
½ cup flour
2 tablespoons oil
½ cup hoisin sauce
½ cup soy sauce
½ cup Chinese rice wine OR dry sherry
½ cup Maui raw sugar
1 teaspoon Chinese five-spice
½ teaspoon ground white pepper

Hāna Fresh Farm Mixed Cherry and Grape Tomato Crostini

Yield: 4 servings

8 slices fresh Italian
    ciabatta bread (1-inch-
    thick slices)
2 tablespoons olive oil
2 cloves garlic, peeled

For the topping:
1 cup mixed cherry and
    grape tomatoes
2 tablespoons minced Kula
    onion
1 teaspoon chopped garlic
2 tablespoons fresh basil
    chiffonade
2 tablespoons chopped
    green olives
2 teaspoons capers
1 teaspoon olive oil
1 teaspoon balsamic
    vinegar
¼ teaspoon sea salt
⅛ teaspoon freshly ground
    pepper

*H*āna Fresh Farms supports and promotes a healthy lifestyle for their community. The produce grown on their farm is free of chemical fertilizers, pesticides, and herbicides and is picked daily. The tomatoes we use in this recipe come from their wonderful farm and are unbelievably sweet.

To prepare the topping, cut the cherry tomatoes into quarters. Prepare the onion, garlic, basil, and green olives per the ingredients list.

Preheat the oven to 400 degrees.

Lightly brush both sides of the bread slices with olive oil. Arrange the slices on a sheet pan. Put the bread in the oven and toast; this should take about 3 to 4 minutes.

Cut the peeled garlic cloves in half and rub the cloves on the toasted bread.

PRESENTATION

Arrange the toast on a platter or on individual serving plates. Spoon the tomato mixture over the toasted bread slices.

Ginger Hoisin Hibachi Rack of Haleakalā Lamb

Yield: 4 to 6 servings

2 lamb racks, approximately 14 to 16 ounces each

For the marinade:
2 tablespoons finely chopped green onion
2 tablespoons peeled and minced ginger
1 cup hoisin sauce
1 cup mirin
½ cup oyster sauce
½ cup water
¼ cup soy sauce
1 teaspoon sambal oelek (Indonesian chili paste)

When you are grilling whole lamb racks, make sure your fire isn't too hot. If it's too hot, the lamb will burn on the outside and remain raw on the inside. Light your coals on your barbecue, then let the fire cool down until your coals become lightly covered with ash. This should be an ideal temperature to begin grilling your lamb. Ask your butcher for Frenched racks with the chine bone removed. You can find sambal oelek or chili and garlic paste at the newly renovated VIP's Foodservices Cash N' Carry store, which carries many unique items.

Chop the green onion and ginger per the ingredients list; mix all the ingredients for the marinade in a large baking dish.

Trim all but a thin layer of fat from the lamb. Score the fat side of each rack in a crosshatch pattern. Put the racks in the baking dish and coat with the marinade. Cover the dish with a lid or with plastic wrap. Refrigerate at least 8 hours or overnight. Turn racks occasionally for even marination.

Fire up your hibachi or charcoal grill until the coals are ready. Grill the lamb racks over medium-heat coals for 5 to 6 minutes on each side. Test the meat with an instant-read meat thermometer to be sure that it's fully cooked; the thermometer, inserted into the center (but not touching bone), should read 120 degrees for medium-rare or 125 degrees for medium.

When the meat is done, remove the meat from the grill and cover it with an aluminum foil tent. Let it rest for 5 minutes before slicing it into chops and serving.

Long Eggplant Stuffed with Shrimp and Black Bean Sauce

*T*he eggplant for this recipe comes from Bryan Otani Farms in Upcountry Kula. Rows of this beautiful vegetable from the nightshade family grow parallel to string beans on the Otani Farm. When choosing the right eggplant, make sure the diameter is no larger than 1½ inches. The eggplant should be firm with unwrinkled and unblemished skin.

To make the sauce, put the chicken broth, black bean garlic sauce, and sugar in a saucepan over medium-high heat. Bring to a boil. Mix the cornstarch and water together until smooth; stir the cornstarch slurry into the sauce. Reduce the heat to medium or medium-low, simmer and stir for approximately 1 minute, or until the sauce thickens. Turn off the heat and set the sauce aside.

Prepare the shrimp, bamboo shoots, water chestnuts, and green onions per the instructions in the ingredients list. Put all the ingredients for the filling in a bowl and mix well.

Cut off the ends of the eggplants, but leave on the skin. Cut the eggplants, on the diagonal, into slices ¾-inch thick. Cut each slice in half again, but without cutting completely through the slice. This makes a pocket for the filling. Fill each eggplant slice with some of the shrimp mixture.

Heat a few teaspoons of vegetable oil in a frying pan over medium heat. When the oil is hot, add the stuffed eggplant slices, cover the pan, and cook for 3 to 4 minutes. Remove the cover, turn the slices, and cook, covered, for another 3 to 4 minutes.

PRESENTATION

Transfer the stuffed eggplant to a serving platter or individual plates; drizzle the sauce over the top or pool on one side. Serve immediately.

Yield: 4 to 6 servings

1 pound Japanese long
   eggplant
Oil for frying

For the filling:
1 pound (21/25) shrimp,
   cleaned, peeled,
   deveined, and finely
   minced
4 tablespoons finely diced
   bamboo shoots
2 tablespoons finely diced
   water chestnuts
2 tablespoons finely
   chopped green onions
2 tablespoons rice wine
2 tablespoons sesame oil
2 tablespoons cornstarch
1 egg white
1 teaspoon sugar
1 teaspoon salt
¼ teaspoon white pepper

For the sauce:
1½ cups chicken broth
4 tablespoons black bean
   garlic sauce (Lee Kum
   Kee brand)
1 tablespoon sugar
2 tablespoons cornstarch
2 tablespoons cold water

Maui Brewing Company Bikini Blonde Beer-Battered Maui Onion Rings

Yield: 4 to 6 servings

2 large Maui onions, cut in
   1-inch rings

For the batter:
1½ cups all-purpose flour
½ cup cornstarch
1 egg, beaten
1 tablespoon Volcano Spice
   or Cajun spice
1 tablespoon kosher salt
2 cups Maui Brewing
   Company Bikini Blonde
   Beer
Oil for deep frying

Upcountry Kula's perfect weather and rich volcanic soil are ideal growing conditions for the sweet onion bulb. Kula onions are celebrated at the annual Maui Onion Festival, held since 1990 in Lahaina. Thousands of visitors and Maui residents gather annually to enjoy tastings, celebrity cooking demonstrations, dinners, and shows. Fried Maui onion rings are one of the festival favorites. Here is my favorite recipe, made with local beer batter.

Mix the all-purpose flour, cornstarch, and salt in a medium-sized bowl. Beat in the egg and add the beer. Whisk until just mixed; don't over-mix, or you will develop the gluten in the flour and your batter will be tough. Let the batter rest for 30 minutes in the refrigerator.

While the batter is chilling, peel the onions and cut them into 1-inch rings. You will probably end up with some slivers of onion that aren't rings; you can save those to use in other dishes.

Heat your deep-fryer or a deep pot full of oil to 350 degrees. A frying thermometer will help you keep the temperature steady.

Dip onion rings into the batter until they are well-covered. Slide a few rings into the oil; don't overcrowd the pot, which will reduce the oil temperature and lead to heavy, greasy rings. Fry the rings until brown and crisp, about 3 to 4 minutes; turn the rings with tongs so that they brown evenly. Remove the cooked rings and let them drain on paper towels.

PRESENTATION
Sprinkle the rings with salt and serve with garlic peppercorn ketchup.

Hāna Baby Cucumber Namasu with Crab and Ogo

This simple namasu recipe features the crisp taste of our Hāna-grown, organic, baby English cucumbers, spiked with the crunch of ogo grown by Island aquaculturalists. Shredded crab meat adds a touch of luxury.

Cut the cucumbers into thin ⅛-inch slices. Put the sliced cucumbers in a bowl and toss them with the kosher salt. Let them sit at room temperature for 20 minutes; the salt will draw some of the water from the cucumber.

While the cucumber is wilting, peel and grate the ginger; rinse and chop the ogo. Mix the rice vinegar, sugar, mirin, and grated ginger in a bowl or container.

When the cucumbers are wilted, put them in a colander and rinse under running water to remove excess salt. Squeeze them lightly with your hands or roll them in a towel to remove even more water.

Add the drained cucumber and chopped ogo to the vinegar mixture and stir to coat. Let the namasu marinate in the refrigerator for at least 30 minutes. Just before serving, add the king crab meat.

Yield: 8 to 10 servings

2 pounds Hāna baby cucumber
1 tablespoon kosher salt
1 teaspoon peeled and grated ginger
½ cup chopped ogo (1-inch pieces)
1 cup rice vinegar
1 cup sugar
1 tablespoon mirin
1 cup shredded king crab leg meat

Neighborhood Farm Organic Egg Frittatas

Yield: 4 to 6 servings

6 organic eggs
½ cup milk
¼ teaspoon salt
⅛ teaspoon pepper

For the tasty bits:
1 cup shredded Cheddar
cheese
1 cup diced Portuguese
sausage (¼-inch dice)
¼ cup drained and chopped
kim chee
2 tablespoons finely sliced
green onions
¼ cup cooked, ½-inch diced
Moloka'i sweet potato
(boiled and peeled)

*N*eighborhood Farm raises fruit, vegetables, and free-range chickens on a small farm just outside Lahaina. They even deliver! Owner Theo Morrison also sells organic eggs, which star in this delicious frittata. When it comes to Portuguese sausage, we like the Nō Ka 'Oi brand. But you're free to use your favorite brand.

Preheat oven to 350 degrees. Grease 12 muffin cups.

Prepare the sweet potato as per the ingredient list.

Shred the cheese, dice and fry the sausage, drain and chop the kim chee, slice the green onion.

Put the eggs, milk, salt, and pepper in a bowl and whisk together. Add the tasty bits and mix well.

Divide the frittata mixture evenly among the 12 greased muffin cups. Bake for 20 minutes at 350 degrees. Remove the individual frittatas from the muffin cups and serve warm.

Makai Catch

Maui families, both Hawaiian and local, have been fishing our waters for hundreds of years. They know the fishing grounds, the seasons, the weather, the water. They know to take only what their family and neighbors need. They throw back the small fish and mālama the ocean for future generations.

Those of us who can eat the Maui catch are so lucky. Our seafood is truly fresh, not unloaded from a trawler that has been fishing for a month and storing the catch on ice. What I like most about fresh fish is that it's so versatile. There are so many ways to cook it, and so many sauces and marinades that you can prepare. But I always remember to treat this important resource with respect. Here are a few recipes that showcase the wonderful and varied Maui seafood.

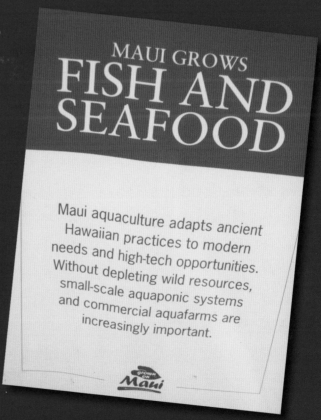

MAUI GROWS
FISH AND SEAFOOD

Maui aquaculture adapts ancient Hawaiian practices to modern needs and high-tech opportunities. Without depleting wild resources, small-scale aquaponic systems and commercial aquafarms are increasingly important.

grown on Maui

'Ahi on the Rock

Yield: 4 servings

12 ounces sashimi-grade
  'ahi, cut into pieces
  approximately 2 inches
  wide by 1 inch high by ¾
  inch thick
2 teaspoons macadamia
  nut oil
1 teaspoon Hawaiian salt
1 teaspoon shichimi pepper
  or to taste
½ teaspoon black sesame
  seeds
12 bamboo or stainless
  steel skewers

For the orange-miso sauce:
1 teaspoon grated ginger
1 tablespoon aka miso
1 tablespoon tahini
¼ cup orange juice
1 tablespoon sesame oil
1 tablespoon soy sauce
1 tablespoon honey

For the garnish:
4 shiso leaves, whole
2 tablespoons pickled
  ginger
¼ cup daikon, julienned
  and rinsed in cold water

This recipe was developed for The Fairmont Kea Lani's plantation-inspired restaurant, Kō. We serve seasoned cubes of fresh island 'ahi with a luscious orange-miso sauce. The food comes to the table with a piping-hot ishiyaki stone (Japanese cooking stone) on a bed of Hawaiian rock salt in a bamboo bowl. Patrons can sear the 'ahi cubes on the heated stone until the fish is just to their taste—lightly seared or completely cooked.

Cooking with hot stones is an old Japanese tradition. There are restaurants in Japan that specialize in ishiyaki cooking. Japanese immigrants brought this delicious tradition to Hawai'i. Ishiyaki stones aren't expensive. However, if you don't want to invest in a stone, you can use a tabletop grill or even an electric frying pan. You can also sear the fish in the kitchen, in a hot cast-iron skillet, and bring it out to your family or guests. Ask them how they want their 'ahi and do your best to serve the right mix of lightly seared and fully cooked pieces.

If you do buy and use an ishiyaki stone, be careful washing it. Let it cool completely, do not wash it with detergent, and do NOT soak the stone. All it needs is a quick scrub and rinse. When heating the stone, use tongs and spatula to move it from the oven or the burner to a heat-proof plate or a large heat-proof bowl filled with Hawaiian rock salt. We heat the stone under the oven broiler or open-flame burner and move it safely with tongs and a spatula.

If you are going to skewer the 'ahi cubes on bamboo skewers, you should soak the bamboo in water for at least 30 minutes before cooking. OR, you can use stainless steel skewers, which don't need soaking.

To make the sauce, peel and grate the ginger. Put all ingredients in a small bowl and whisk together. Cover the bowl and chill the sauce in the refrigerator until it is time to serve the fish.

To prepare the garnish, wash the shiso leaves. Drain the pickled ginger and julienne the daikon. Rinse in cold water then drain and set aside.

Cut the 'ahi into pieces approximately 2 inches wide by 1 inch high by ¾ inch thick.

(recipe continued on page 58)

Brush the cut 'ahi cubes with macadamia nut oil and season them with Hawaiian salt and shichimi pepper to taste. Sprinkle the black sesame seeds on the fish.

If you are using an ishiyaki stone, thread each 'ahi cube on a bamboo or metal skewer. Heat the ishiyaki stone in your oven under the broiler or over a burner. It can take high heat, so feel free to heat it over an open gas flame. Use tongs and a spatula to move the stone to a heat-proof plate or a heat-proof ceramic bowl filled with Hawaiian rock salt.

If using a cast-iron frying pan in the kitchen, heat the pan over high heat and quickly sear the cubes on all sides. Tongs or cooking chopsticks will help you manage the cubes.

PRESENTATION

Fill 4 small sauce dishes with orange-miso sauce. Divide the garnish among 4 plates. Put 1 dish of sauce and 1 plate of garnish with pickled ginger, shiso, and daikon at each setting.

If using an ishiyaki stone, bring the heated stone and the chunks of raw fish to the table. Let your family or guests sear the fish to their taste. If using a cast-iron skillet in the kitchen, bring the seared cubes to the table on a serving platter.

Lobster Cakes with Red Thai Curry Sauce

*T*his is my version of crab cakes. If you can't find freshly caught local lobster, frozen ones will do fine. The sauce is classic Thai red curry sauce instead of a Cajun mayonnaise. If you can't find palm sugar at the supermarket, you can substitute brown sugar.

To make the sauce, peel and mince the shallots. Cut the kaffir lime leaf into thin slivers. Pull off the tough outer leaves of the lemongrass and discard; cut off and discard the very end of the lower bulb. Thinly slice the bottom ⅔ of the stalk. The top ⅓ of the stalk may be too woody to use in sauce, but you may want to save it to add flavor to a broth or stew (pound or slice it to release the flavors, add it to the broth, and remove it before serving). Pound the sliced lemongrass in a mortar or process it briefly in a food processor, to further break down the fibers.

Heat the peanut oil in a frying pan or saucepan over medium-high heat. Add the shallots, lemongrass, and curry paste. Sauté the mixture for 3 minutes or until fragrant. Add the slivers of kaffir lime leaf and the cup of coconut milk. Bring the sauce to a boil. Turn the heat to low, season with the fish sauce and sugar, and cook briefly. Turn off the heat and cover.

To make the lobster cakes, chop the lobster meat and the cilantro. Place the lobster, cilantro, egg, panko, mayonnaise, Worcesteshire sauce, and Tabasco sauce in a bowl and mix well.

Form the lobster mixture into 8 patties. Heat the vegetable oil in a large frying pan over medium heat. Add the patties to the pan and sauté until lightly browned on both sides.

PRESENTATION

Serve the cakes on a pool of Thai red curry sauce.

Yield: 4 servings

For the lobster cakes:
1 pound frozen lobster tail meat, chopped (spiny lobster, Maine lobster or slipper lobster will all work; defrost in the refrigerator or run under cold water)
1 tablespoon chopped cilantro
1 large egg, beaten
½ cup panko flakes
5 tablespoons mayonnaise
2 teaspoons Worcestershire sauce
4 to 5 drops Tabasco sauce
Salt to taste
Vegetable oil for sautéing

For the Thai red curry sauce:
½ tablespoon finely minced shallots
1 kaffir lime leaf, de-ribbed and cut into thin slivers
½ tablespoon minced lemongrass
2 tablespoons peanut oil
1 tablespoon Thai red curry paste
1 cup coconut milk
2 teaspoons fish sauce
2 teaspoons palm sugar or brown sugar

Wok-Seared Monchong with Black Bean Sauce

*C*hinese chefs use douchi, fermented black beans, to add a piquant touch to many dishes. You can buy black bean sauces in bottles at the supermarket but for the best taste, I recommend that you make your own sauce from scratch. In this recipe, the sauce complements some wok-fried monchong. If you like the taste, you may want to try your homemade sauce with other fish dishes or with Chinese-style spareribs. This is my dad, Yun Young Pang's, version of black bean sauce. You can substitute a soft textured white fish. Monchong can only be found in Hawaiian waters. Its high oil content preserves moisture and offers a unique deep buttery flavor.

To make the sauce, rinse and drain the fermented black beans. Mince the garlic and ginger. Heat the oil in a small saucepan over medium heat; add the black beans, garlic, ginger, and chili flakes and sauté until fragrant. Add the chicken stock, oyster sauce, sugar, and salt. Raise the heat slightly and bring the mixture to a boil. Turn the heat down to medium-low. Mix the cornstarch and water into a smooth paste. Add the cornstarch slurry to the sauce and stir until the sauce thickens. Remove the sauce from the heat and cover to retain heat.

Season monchong fillets with salt and pepper to your taste. Dredge fish in the flour; shake off any excess. Heat the oil in a large frying pan over medium-high heat. When the oil is hot, add the fish and cook for 3 minutes on each side, or until the fish is cooked. It will no longer be opaque and will be starting to stiffen. Fish continues to cook even after you remove it from the pan, so it is best to slightly undercook the fish and let it finish cooking on the plate.

PRESENTATION

Place fish on a serving platter and ladle black bean sauce over the top. Garnish with the sliced green onions.

Yield: 4 servings

4 (5-ounce) monchong fillets
Salt and pepper to season
4 tablespoons flour
2 tablespoons oil

For the black bean sauce:
2 tablespoons fermented black beans, rinsed and drained
1 clove garlic, minced
1 teaspoon minced ginger
¼ teaspoon red chili flakes
1 tablespoon oil
¾ cup chicken stock
2 tablespoons oyster sauce
1 teaspoon sugar
½ teaspoon salt

For the cornstarch slurry:
2 teaspoons cornstarch
1 tablespoon cold water

For the garnish:
1 tablespoon finely sliced green onions

Macadamia Nut-Crusted Mahimahi with Olowalu Nui Tomato and Ginger

Yield: 4 servings

2 tablespoons melted
butter
4 (5-ounce) mahimahi fillets
Salt and pepper to taste

For the nut crust:
½ cup finely chopped
macadamia nuts
½ teaspoon chopped
parsley
½ cup panko (Japanese-
style bread crumbs)
½ teaspoon paprika

*For the tomato ginger
sauce:*
1 cup seeded and diced
(¼-inch) tomato
¼ cup finely diced Maui
onion
1 tablespoon finely sliced
green onions
2 teaspoons finely minced
pickled ginger
2 tablespoons olive oil
4 tablespoons butter
Salt and pepper to taste

It's our responsibility to support our local fishermen and farmers. I always use fish from Maui waters and local produce whenever possible—like Olowalu tomatoes, which are fresher and sweeter because they are kept on the vines longer. Adding pickled ginger adds a new twist.

Preheat the oven to 400 degrees.

To make the nut crust, chop the nuts and parsley per the instructions in the ingredients list. Mix the nuts, parsley, panko, and paprika in a shallow pan and set aside.

To make the sauce, prepare the tomato, onion, green onions, and ginger per the ingredients list. Heat the olive oil in a sauté pan over medium heat; add the chopped onion and cook until soft. Add the diced tomatoes and pickled ginger and cook for 1 to 2 minutes. Whisk in the butter. When it has melted, turn off the heat under the pan and add the green onions. Season with salt and pepper to taste. Cover the sauce to retain heat.

Melt the butter in a small saucepan or the microwave. Season the mahimahi fillets with salt and pepper. Coat the fillets with the nut crust mixture. Put the fillets in a baking pan and drizzle with the melted butter. Bake the fillets in the 400 degree oven until the crust is nicely browned, about 10 minutes.

PRESENTATION

Serve the cooked fish on top of the finished tomato and ginger sauce.

Maui Fishermen

We'd like to send a big mahalo to John Keanaaina, Doug Muller, Gilbert Edo, Alan Cadiz, Eunice Lind, Salvador Santos, Daniel Goldberg, Shawn Boneza, and all the other Maui fishermen who bring so much passion and heart to their work. These guys really love the ocean, and they understand what it means to take care of it—they fish sustainably, and are careful to bring back only what they can eat and share, so that all the creatures in our Hawaiian waters have a chance to grow and thrive. These fishermen have a good time going out and doing what they love, and we—and our bellies—are very grateful to them!

Tangled Tiger Prawns with Pineapple-Chili-Garlic Sauce

Yield: 4 servings

12 each (21/15) tiger
  prawns, peeled and
  deveined
4 ounce katafi (shredded
  phyllo dough)
1 teaspoon sake
1 teaspoon lime juice
½ teaspoon salt
Oil for deep-frying

*For the pineapple-chili-
garlic sauce:*
½ cup pineapple, diced
  (¼-inch)
1 tablespoon minced Maui
  onion
2 cloves garlic, finely
  chopped
1 tablespoon chopped
  cilantro
½ cup sugar
½ cup rice wine vinegar
1 teaspoon sambal oelek
  (Indonesian chili paste)

The Taste of Lahaina festival is an annual event featuring restaurant booths serving toothsome samples, live music, and rides for the keiki and young at heart. It's Maui's favorite culinary event. Where else can you sample and compare food from the best restaurants on the island? Restaurants showcase their tastiest recipes here and hope to win. This recipe, we're proud to say, debuted at the festival and won both the best seafood and best of show categories. The sauce compliments this dish as the vinegar will cut the oil. This unique sweet-and-sour sauce can be used with other fried foods, including spring rolls, and chicken.

To make the sauce, cut up the pineapple, onion, garlic, and cilantro per the instructions in the ingredients list. Put the pineapple, onion, garlic, sugar, vinegar, and sambal oelek in a saucepan over medium-high heat and bring to a boil for 2 minutes. Remove from the heat and let cool. Stir in the chopped cilantro just before serving.

Marinate the prawns with the sake, lime juice, and salt for 20 minutes.

Thread the marinated prawns from the tail end onto each of the (6-inch) bamboo skewers. Divide the shredded phyllo into 12 even strands and lay the skewered prawns at one end of the phyllo strands and wrap around the prawns, tangling them up.

Heat oil in your deep-fryer or a deep pot to 350 degrees. Deep-fry the skewered prawns for 1½ to 2 minutes, or until they are golden brown. You will probably have to do this in several batches; don't crowd the oil. Drain the prawns on paper towels.

PRESENTATION

Divide the chili-garlic sauce into small bowls and serve alongside these crispy prawn skewers.

Grilled Opah with Miso Butter

*O*pah, Hawaiian moonfish, used to be considered a trash fish. 'Ahi fishermen would throw it back or use it for bait. Then Sam Choy, one of Hawai'i's most famous chefs, popularized opah with a few of his tasty recipes. Now opah commands top dollar and can be found on the menu at Maui's finest restaurants.

To make the miso butter, peel and mince a slice or two of Maui onion. You only need a teaspoonful. Put the onion and white wine in a small saucepan over medium heat. Simmer the mixture until the wine is reduced by a third. Add the cream and reduce by a third again. Reduce the heat to low and stir in the miso paste. Slowly whisk in the butter, one cube at a time. Season with salt and pepper to taste.

Fire up your gas or charcoal grill. Brush the opah filets with olive oil and season to taste with salt and pepper. Grill the fish 3 to 4 minutes on each side, or until the fish is done to your liking.

PRESENTATION

Serve the fish on a platter or individual plates. Drizzle miso sauce over the fish. Serve with the wedges of fresh lime.

Yield: 4 servings

4 (5-ounce) opah fillets
2 teaspoons olive oil
Salt and pepper to season

For the miso butter:
1 teaspoon minced Maui
   onion
¼ cup white wine
¼ cup cream
1 tablespoon aka miso
4 tablespoons butter, cut
   into ½-inch cubes

For the garnish:
1 fresh lime, cut into 4
   wedges

Ginger-Steamed Kūmū with Chinese Sausage

Yield: 2 to 3 servings

1½ pounds kūmū, scaled and cleaned

3 each lup cheong (Chinese sausage, about 4 ounces), thinly sliced on the diagonal

1 tablespoon chung choi (salted turnip), rinsed and minced

1 tablespoon julienned ginger

1 teaspoon salt

2 tablespoons soy sauce

2 tablespoons peanut oil

1 teaspoon oyster sauce

For the garnish:

4 green onion stalks, sliced on the diagonal

1 small bunch cilantro, cut into sprigs

It's a Chinese tradition to serve fish cooked whole; the fish is a symbol of good luck and prosperity. This steamed fish is extra lucky, because it's red, the color of happiness. Double benefits! How could you go wrong serving this? I learned this recipe from my dad and fond memories of family gatherings always come back when I prepare this dish. You can substitute moi or mullet.

P.S. Also, it's delicious!

Slice the lup cheong and the chung choi per the instructions in the ingredients list. Peel and julienne the ginger.

Fill the bottom of a tiered steamer (or a large pot with steamer insert) with water and bring it to a boil over high heat. If you don't have a steamer, you can improvise one with a large pot and a stand that will lift the plate of fish slightly above the level of the water.

Place cleaned kūmū in an attractive heat-proof serving dish. Season with salt and chung choi. Arrange the ginger and lup cheong slices on top of the fish.

Put the plate of fish in the steamer and steam for 20 minutes. Check the water occasionally to make sure that the steamer doesn't boil dry.

While the fish is steaming, mix the soy sauce and oyster sauce in a small bowl. Cut up the green onions and cilantro for the garnish.

Remove the fish from the steamer. Pour the soy and oyster sauce mixture over the fish. Garnish with the green onion and cilantro.

Heat the peanut oil in a small saucepan over high heat. When the oil has just started to smoke, carefully drizzle it over the fish. Serve the fish immediately.

Spicy 'Ahi Won Ton Cones

Spicy 'ahi poke fills crisp won ton cones. A lovely contrast of textures! If you roll won ton wrappers into cones and drop them in hot oil, they will fall apart. You won't end up with cones. The trick is to wrap the won ton wrapper around a cornet mold, which is approximately 5½ inches long and 1¼ inches in diameter at the top, and use a second mold to hold the wrapper in place while you fry it crispy. Fry the cone sandwich, remove from the oil, remove the pastry cones, and voilà! A perfectly shaped won ton cone.

You may not have two or more large pastry cones. If not, deep-fry the whole won ton wrappers. Serve the minced 'ahi on the chips. The dish won't be as visually appealing, but it will still be 'onolicious.

Mince the 'ahi and green onion. Mix the 'ahi, onion, shichimi, sesame oil, and salt. Cover and set in the refrigerator to chill.

Put the wasabi powder in a small bowl and mix with a few drops of water to make a paste. Add the mayonnaise to the wasabi paste and mix well. Cover and set in the refrigerator to chill.

If you're making won ton cones, fold a won ton wrapper over a pastry cone. Hold in place with a second cone.

Heat the oil in your deep-fryer or a deep pot to 350 degrees. Fry the cone sandwich and drain it on paper towels. Remove the pastry cones and shape another wrapper. Continue frying until all the cones are fried. (If you have more than 2 pastry cones, you can fry several cones at the same time.)

If you're not making cones, drop a won ton wrapper into the oil, fry till crisp, and drain. Repeat until all the wrappers have been fried.

PRESENTATION

Place a shiso leaf in each won ton cone or in the center of each wrapper. Divide the spicy tuna mix into 8 equal portions and spoon into the cones or on the wrappers. Garnish each serving with some of the wasabi mayonnaise and a dab of tobiko. Serve immediately, while the won ton wrappers are still crisp.

Yield: 4 servings

½ pound sashimi-grade 'ahi, minced
1 tablespoon minced green onion
½ teaspoon shichimi red pepper mix
1 tablespoon sesame oil
1 teaspoon sea salt
2 tablespoons mayonnaise
1 teaspoon wasabi powder
1 tablespoon orange tobiko (flying fish roe)
8 shiso leaves
8 won ton wrappers
oil for deep-frying

Sake-Glazed Ehu

Yield: 6 servings

6 (5-ounce) ehu fillets,
scaled with skin on
2 tablespoons peanut oil

Garnish:
12 spears Anuhea Farms
asparagus
1 sheet yaki nori (crisp
squares of seaweed), cut
into strips
1 cup julienned daikon
½ cup julienned carrot
1 teaspoon toasted sesame
seeds
1 tablespoon finely sliced
green onions

For the sake glaze:
¼ cup soy sauce
¼ cup mirin
¼ cup sugar
2 tablespoons sake

Ehu, the short-tail red snapper, isn't as popular as its cousin the 'ōpakapaka, the pink snapper. Locals know that ehu is just as tasty as 'ōpakapaka and don't hesitate to buy it when it's available.

Peel and cut carrots and daikon into julienne strips. Rinse in cold water and drain. Cut the ends of the asparagus and blanch in boiling salted water for 30 seconds. Cool in ice water then drain. Reserve these vegetables on the side to garnish the finished dish. Cut the yaki nori sheets into four even strips, then stack and use scissors to cut into fine julienne strips.

To make the glaze, mix all ingredients in a small bowl; stir until all the sugar has dissolved.

Heat the peanut oil in a sauté pan over medium-high heat. The oil should be hot, on the verge of smoking. Quickly sear the ehu on both sides. Lower the heat, pour the sake glaze over the fish, and continue cooking the fish while continually spooning glaze from the bottom of the pan and drizzling it over the fish. Continue this process until the fish is cooked (opaque and firm) and evenly glazed. The sauce should be reduced to a syrup-like consistency.

PRESENTATION

Arrange the julienned carrots and daikon onto serving platters in mounds and place the cooked ehu leaning against the vegetables. Place cooked asparagus spears on the filets, and garnish with the finely cut yaki nori strips, toasted sesame seeds, and sliced green onions.

Kaku Katsu with Pickled Ginger and Shiso Aioli

veryday fried fish is glorious when paired with the piquant tastes of pickled ginger and shiso leaves. Kaku or baraccuda is a common catch of local fishermen although it's a fierce predator and quite a handful when caught on a hook and line. Kaku is more of a family food. Fishermen are not always able to sell it so it, ends up more on their dinner table than in fish markets. This is my version of tartar sauce.

To make the aioli, chop the ginger and shiso leaves. Mix the ginger, shiso, mayonnaise, soy sauce, sambal, and sesame oil and set aside.

Line up three shallow pans, large enough to hold one of the kaku fillets. Measure the flour into one pan, beat the eggs in another, and put the panko in the last. This is your breading station.

Season the kaku with salt, pepper, Worcestershire sauce, and lemon juice. Dredge the seasoned fish in the flour, then dip in the beaten egg, and finally coat it evenly with the panko.

Cover the bottom of a large frying pan with vegetable oil and heat over medium-high heat. When the oil is hot, add the kaku fillets and fry until evenly browned on both sides. This should take about 3 minutes on each side. Drain the fillets on paper towels.

PRESENTATION

Arrange the fillets on a serving platter and serve with pickled ginger and shiso aioli on the side.

Yield: 4 servings

4 (5-ounce) kaku fillets
½ teaspoon salt
¼ teaspoon pepper
½ teaspoon Worcestershire sauce
½ teaspoon lemon juice
½ cup flour
2 eggs, beaten
1 cup panko (Japanese-style bread crumbs)
Vegetable oil for frying

For the pickled ginger and shiso aioli:
1 tablespoon finely minced pickled ginger
4 shiso leaves, finely chopped
¼ cup mayonnaise
1 teaspoon soy sauce
1 teaspoon sambal oelek (Indonesian chili paste)
½ teaspoon sesame oil

Timmy with barracuda

Crispy Moi with Sweet-and-Sour Sauce

Yield: 2 servings

1 whole moi (thread fin)
   (about 1½ to 2 pounds,
   scaled and cleaned, dry)
1 tablespoon rice wine
1 teaspoon sea salt
½ cup flour
½ cup cornstarch
2 eggs, beaten
Oil for deep-frying

*For the sweet-and-sour
   sauce:*
4 shiitake mushrooms,
   julienned
¼ cup Maui onions,
   julienned
2 green onion stalks, cut on
   the diagonal
1 clove garlic, minced
¼ cup bell peppers,
   julienned
¼ cup carrots, julienned
2 tablespoons vegetable oil
¼ cup rice vinegar
¼ cup sugar
3 tablespoons ketchup
1 tablespoon rice wine
1 tablespoon soy sauce
1 tablespoon sesame oil

For the cornstarch slurry:
5 tablespoons cornstarch
½ cup cold water

In olden times, the moi was reserved for the chiefs. Now it's available to everyone, thanks to local aquaculture farms. Try some of this delicious fish and you'll see why chiefs craved it so.

Hawaiian wisdom: Local fishermen know it is a good moi season when there are many mango flowers on the mango tree.

To make the sauce, cut up the mushrooms, onions, green onions, garlic, bell peppers, and carrots per the instructions in the ingredients list.

Heat the 2 tablespoons of vegetable oil in a large shallow pan over medium-high heat. When the oil is hot, add the onions, garlic, and carrots. When those have softened, add the mushrooms and bell peppers.

When the vegetables have softened, add the rice vinegar, sugar, ketchup, rice wine, soy sauce, and sesame oil, and bring to a boil. Lower the heat slightly. Mix the cornstarch and water to form a smooth paste. Add the cornstarch slurry and stir while the sauce thickens. Turn off the heat and cover the sauce.

To cook the fish, make 3 diagonal slits on both sides of the moi. Rub the rice wine over the fish. Sprinkle the fish with sea salt.

Mix the flour and cornstarch in a shallow pan large enough to hold the fish. Beat the eggs in another shallow pan of the same size. Dredge the fish in the flour mixture, dip it into the beaten eggs, and then dredge it in the flour again.

Pour oil into a wok until you have enough oil to cover the fish. Heat the oil until a deep-frying thermometer registers 350 degrees. Add the fish and fry it for 10 to 12 minutes, turning the fish once at the 5- or 6-minute mark. Remove the fish from the oil and drain it on paper towels.

PRESENTATION

Serve the fish piping hot, with the sweet-and-sour sauce and vegetables over the top. Garnish with the cut green onions.

Maui Lavender Honey Macadamia Nut Shrimp

We presented this dish at Kaua'i's Taste of Hawai'i festival in 2009. It was voted best in the Seafood category. It's my version of the classic Chinese Honey Walnut Shrimp dish.

Defrost and drain the shrimp. The shrimp should be as dry as possible—no excess water. Put rice wine, sesame oil, egg white, and salt in a bowl and mix well. Add the shrimp and let it marinate for 30 minutes. Drain the shrimp again.

While the shrimp are marinating, make the honey sauce. Just mix all the ingredients in a bowl. Cover and set aside.

Place a sheet or two of waxed paper on top of a sheet pan with shallow sides. Put some cornstarch in a shallow pan. Dredge the marinated shrimp in the cornstarch; dust off any excess. Place the shrimp on the waxed paper, being careful not to overlap any shrimp. Put the shrimp in the refrigerator for 20 minutes, or until the cornstarch is moist. This will prevent the coating from falling off while you are deep-frying the shrimp.

While the shrimp are cooling, make the candied macadamia nuts. Boil the macadamia nuts with sugar and water for 10 minutes. Drain all the liquid.

Heat the oil in your deep-fryer or a deep pot until it is 350 degrees. Deep-fry the nuts until golden-brown and drain on paper towels. (If you have a deep-frying basket, use it for easy lowering and lifting.)

Now slip a batch of shrimp into the oil and fry until crisp and golden in color. This should take about 2 minutes. Remove that batch of shrimp and drain it on paper towels. Repeat until all the shrimp are fried.

PRESENTATION

Toss the shrimp in the honey sauce. Top with candied macadamia nuts and serve on a bed of Kula greens.

Yield: 6 servings

2 pounds (21/25) shrimp, peeled and deveined, tail off
2 teaspoons shao xing (rice wine) OR dry sherry
2 teaspoons sesame oil
1 egg white
1 teaspoon sea salt
2 cups cornstarch for dredging
Oil for deep-frying

For the honey sauce:
¼ cup Ali'i Kula lavender honey
2 tablespoons sweetened condensed milk
½ cup mayonnaise
1 tablespoon lemon juice

For the candied nuts:
1 cup water
1 cup sugar
½ cup macadamia nuts

Garnish:
2 cups of fresh Kula green salad, cut and washed

Ocean Treasures

Here are some recipes for seafood dishes that you probably won't find in your local supermarket or fish market. In fact, these delicacies are so special and specific to Maui that you probably won't find them anywhere else in the world. If you don't fish or gather from the rocks and reefs, or know someone who does, you may just have to read the recipes and dream.

The fishermen who know how to find and cook these seafood treats are old-timers with years and years of fishing experience. I'm not going to tell you where to go—that's their secret—but I do feel responsible for preserving some of the old Maui knowledge. I'm particularly grateful to John Keanaaina, well-known local musician, for sharing his stories of fishing trips with his kūpuna.

Crispy Calamari

Yield: 4 servings

12 ounces (¾ pound)
   frozen calamari rings
   and tentacles, Aqua Star
   brand
½ cup milk
1 cup flour (seasoned with
   salt and pepper)
Oil for deep frying

For the dipping sauce:
¼ cup mayonnaise
1 teaspoon masago (smelt
   eggs, also called capelin
   roe)
½ teaspoon soy sauce
½ teaspoon lemon juice
½ teaspoon honey

For the garnish:
Fresh lettuce leaf, whole,
   as the base for fried
   calamari
Crisp-fried bean threads
Lemon wedges
(Serve with one, two, or all
   three of these garnishes.)

I remember going with my father to catch squid at night. Many fishermen often use squid as bait, and any leftover is then used for cooking if some already hasn't been set aside. If you are not experienced with cleaning fresh squid or can't get any ready to cook from the fish department, use the frozen kind found in supermarkets.

We recommend using Aqua Star brand frozen calamari rings and tentacles that are IQF cleaned, cut, and ready to use. It is available in most grocery stores and has thawing directions. It will be more user friendly for home cooks. Place in refrigerator and thaw overnight or rinse under cold water before using.

Marinate the calamari in milk for 30 minutes. Wash the whole-leaf lettuce, cut a lemon or two into wedges, and open up a small package of bean thread. Separate the threads; you don't want to fry them in a clump. Mix all the ingredients for the dipping sauce, then cover and set aside.

Drain the calamari. Put the flour in a shallow pan and season with salt and pepper. Dredge the calamari in the flour; shake off any excess.

Heat the oil in your deep-fryer or a deep pot to 350 degrees. Deep-fry the calamari until crisp and golden brown. You will probably have to do this in several batches. Drain the calamari on paper towels.

If you are planning to serve the calamari with a fried bean thread garnish, keep the oil hot and fry the bean threads. This will be easier if you have a large stainless steel sieve; you can use it to lower the threads into the oil and remove them when crisp. Drain the threads on paper towels.

PRESENTATION

Divide the dipping sauce among 4 small bowls, or one for each place setting. Serve the calamari on a platter garnished with the whole-leaf lettuce, crisp bean threads, and lemon wedges.

'Ono Squid Lū'au

Yield: 6 servings

2½ pounds taro leaves
(lū'au), cleaned, stems
removed

2 pounds frozen calamari
rings and tentacles, Aqua
Star brand

2 tablespoons baking soda

2 tablespoons Hawaiian salt

1 medium Kula onion, cut
into ¼-inch dice

½ cup butter

3¾ to 4 cups fresh, frozen,
or canned coconut milk

4 tablespoons coconut
syrup

2 teaspoons table salt

(Courtesy of John Keanaaina)

"*When I was growing up, squid was something you ate when you couldn't get he'e, or octopus. He'e live at 20 to 40 foot depths; divers swim down into the he'e ground, startling the octopus. The octopus blush (change color) and give away their location, enabling them to be grabbed or speared. There is no he'e fishing during the winter months, when seas are rough, so fishermen look for squid instead of he'e.*

My area had no he'e grounds. so we cooked with squid—sometimes fresh, sometimes frozen. We would get our fresh squid from the ika-shibi fishermen who went out at night to fish the squid grounds, squid attract big-eye tuna. The fishermen caught the tuna with squid bait. Frozen squid was readily available at the corner market. The market sold a lot of squid as fish bait, but it was good for cooking as well." John Keanaaina

Prepare the taro leaves per the instructions in the ingredient list. Place the calamari rings and tentacles in the refrigerator, and thaw overnight or rinse under cold water before using.

Fill a large pot with water until it is about ⅔ full. Add the baking soda and Hawaiian salt. Bring to a boil. Add the lū'au leaves, a few leaves at a time rather than all at once. Boil the leaves until they fall apart easily when stirred. This will take about 1 hour, more or less. Drain leaves in a large colander or strainer.

Cut up the onion. Melt the butter in a large frying pan over medium heat. Sauté the onion until it wilts and becomes translucent. Be careful not to burn it. Add the cut-up squid and sauté for 1 minute, or until the squid turns white. Remove the pan from the heat.

Put the lū'au leaves back in the large pot and add the sautéed squid and onions.

Mix the coconut milk and coconut syrup in a deep bowl. Add this coconut mixture to the pot full of lū'au leaves with the squid and onions. Mix well. Cook the squid lū'au over low heat for 15 minutes. Remove from heat and serve immediately.

Roasted Leho Kinilau

(Courtesy of John Keanaaina)

Yield: 4 appetizer servings

Ingredients:

- 4 (large to medium) leho (cowry)
- 1 medium Kula onion, finely chopped
- 4 stalks green onion, finely chopped
- 1 large tomato, seeds removed, finely chopped
- 4 fronds hō'i'o fern shoots, finely chopped
- ½ cup limu līpoa, finely chopped
- 1 clove garlic, minced
- 1 (thumb-sized) piece of ginger, peeled and minced
- 1 tablespoon Kula Onion Pepper Water (see recipe on page 89)
- ½ cup soy sauce
- 1 rounded tablespoon Hawaiian salt

*O*nce again, my dear friend John Keanaaina was kind enough to share this recipe and story. Though leho or cowrie is not a common food today, it definitely was considered an ocean treasure.

"While I was growing up, in the late 1950s, 60s, and the early 70s, I was carefully taught how to fish and cook by my kūpuna, my father and uncles. They knew how to catch and prepare the many kinds of seafood found in Hawaiian waters. We made monthly treks, by foot or donkey, to remote beaches. There we would catch, cook, and preserve seafood, enough for a few months. When we had reached our quota, we would pack up what we had prepared and take it back home, where we divided the food evenly between everyone in our 'ohana.

These excursions would last approximately 3 to 4 days; they were carefully timed to take advantage of the best fishing times, as determined by the moon, the tide, and the ocean. During the day, we would net and spearfish, or gather shellfish when the tide was low. At night, we would gather 'a'ama crabs, or fish for nocturnal fish like 'ū'ū, 'upāpalu, moi, 'āweoweo, and 'ala'ihi."

To prepare the leho, light some kiawe charcoal in your hibachi or grill and let the briquets burn until they're covered with grey ash. Now the fire will be ready and slightly cooled to roast the leho. Roast the leho, still in their shells, over the briquets for 15 minutes. Remove them from the heat and let them cool for 15 minutes.

Use a hammer to break the leho shells. Remove the meat from the shells. Clean the meat under running water to remove any shell fragments.

Pat the meat dry with paper towels and refrigerate for 2 hours. Or, you can salt the leho meat and chill it in a closed cooler for 2 hours. (Guess which method John used when fishing on remote beaches.)

Cut up the onion, green onion, tomato, hō'i'o fern, limu līpoa, garlic, and ginger per the instructions in the ingredients list. Thinly slice the leho into pieces.

Mix the soy sauce and the chili pepper water. Mix all ingredients. Refrigerate for 1 to 2 hours, mix again, and serve.

Spicy Tako Poke

Just about everyone loves to eat tako poke (tako being the Japanese name for the he'e, or octopus). Local divers not only love to eat he'e, they love to dive for it. They're always waiting for just the right conditions (calm ocean and low tide) to head out to their favorite he'e grounds. When at the beach, or just driving past the beach, if you see the water dotted with red dive floats and flags, it means that the divers are out in force. Look for them at Kanahā Beach, Ledges, or driving along South Kīhei Road.

Slice the cooked and cleaned tako into ¼-inch slices.

Prepare the onion, green onion, and ginger per the instructions in the ingredients list.

Put all the ingredients in a large bowl and mix well. Cover and chill in the refrigerator for at least 1 hour before serving.

Yield: 6 to 8 servings

2 pounds cooked and
   cleaned tako
½ small Kula onion, ¼-inch
   dice
6 stalks green onion, finely
   chopped
2 teaspoons ginger, peeled
   and grated
2 teaspoons toasted
   sesame seeds
2 teaspoons paprika
¼ teaspoon dried chili
   pepper flakes
½ cup soy sauce
1 tablespoon sesame oil
1 tablespoon honey

Spicy Ogo Salad

Yield: 4 to 6 servings

1 pound ogo seaweed
1 medium Maui onion,
   thinly sliced
3 tablespoons finely
   chopped green onion
3 cloves garlic, minced
½ cup soy sauce
½ cup rice vinegar
4 tablespoons sugar
1 tablespoon sesame oil
½ teaspoon sambal oelek
   (Indonesian chili paste)

Several island aquaculture firms are growing ogo, a delicious crunchy seaweed. This ogo salad is sparked with onion, garlic, and Southeast Asian chili paste.

Clean and rinse the ogo. If the strands are long, give it a rough chop and put it in a heat-proof bowl. Cut up the onion, green onion, and garlic according to the instructions in the ingredients list.

Boil 1 quart of water and pour it over the ogo. Let the ogo sit in the water for 30 seconds, then pour it into a colander to drain.

Mix the blanched ogo with the remaining ingredients. Put in a covered container and leave it to chill in the refrigerator overnight.

John Keanaaina

John Keanaaina is a very rich man.

He grew up in a family with five brothers and sisters and many extended family members. The house was welcoming and full of music, and there was always plenty of food to go around—most of it harvested sustainably from the ocean.

In the winter, when the waves had washed away much of the white sand, John's dad, John Sr., would race his horse along the shoreline, scaring the white crabs out of their holes and up onto the beach, where his family would be waiting to catch them. When everyone got home, they'd make fresh raw crab poke with inamona, Hawaiian salt, and onions—so 'ono!

Sometimes, very early in the morning, Grand-uncle Nuhi would knock on the Keanaainas' door and ask if he could "borrow" the kids for the day. This meant getting out of school and spending the whole day out on Nuhi's canoe, fishing for 'ōpelu. Before setting out, they'd usually drop nets for Kona crabs, substituting a dry coconut or an empty plastic bottle for the floater. And when they got back, John Sr. would be ready with all the ingredients for lomi 'ōpelu.

John Sr. was also an expert fisherman, with great respect for the ocean and the spirits. Once, when throwing net at night, he noticed that the net was shining in the water. The fishing spot was near an ancient burial site. "I going home!" he said loudly, and then drove his truck about ¾-mile down the road. He turned the truck around, and when the family got back to the beach, shine had left the net. The spirits thought they'd left, so they went home too.

Oven-Dried Akule

Yield: 4 servings

4 whole akule,
   approximately 1 pound
   each
1 cup soy sauce
½ cup turbinado sugar
   (Maui raw sugar)
¼ cup mirin
½ teaspoon sesame seeds
¼ teaspoon dried chili
   flakes

The akule, or bigeye scad, is common in Hawaiian waters. It's a schooling fish; if fishermen find a school, they can often catch akule in great numbers. For centuries, Maui's akule fishermen have been netting, scaling, splitting, gutting, and drying their catch, passing their skills from generation to generation. In the olden times, the drying akule would be strung on cords and hung to dry. In modern times, we can dry our fish in an oven.

Scale the fish (scraping from tail to head with a dull knife), and rinse well. Cut each fish in half lengthwise, cutting through the back of the head to the tail, butterflying open. This will require a sharp knife. Spread the two halves of the fish open. Remove the gills and viscera. Rinse lightly and pat dry. Lay the fish, skin-side down, on the wire rack of your roasting pan.

Preheat your oven to 225 degrees.

Mix the soy sauce, sugar, and mirin for the marinade. Baste the top of the fish with the marinade and marinate for 2 hours. Sprinkle the sesame seeds and dried chili flakes over the exposed meat.

Place the rack in your roasting pan. Dry the fish in the 225-degree oven for 4 hours. The dried akule can now be stored in freezer bags and will keep for 1 week in your refrigerator or 1 month in the freezer.

To enjoy your home-dried akule, slide a fish or two under the broiler skin-side up and heat through. It tastes best when the skin gets crispy and a little bubbly—about 3 minutes on each side should do it. You can eat the skin and all. Just be careful of the bones.

Hibachi 'Opihi with Tomato Salsa

'Opihi are limpets that grow on rocks on wave-splashed shores. They're a traditional delicacy in the Islands, and they are being loved to extinction. Most of the 'opihi are gone from rocks that are easy to reach. They are now found mainly in remote, dangerous locations. 'Opihi pickers keep those locations secret, lest they too be picked bare.

You can buy 'opihi (at stratospheric prices) at several fishmarkets. If you know where to go, you can gather your own. Remember, obey the laws! Take only what you need, don't eat them while you're picking, and don't gather the keiki. Any 'opihi smaller than a quarter are too young to gather.

Here's a delicious way to honor these wonderful limpets.

Fire up the grill with kiawe charcoal. While the briquets are getting started, cut up the onion, green onion, tomato, ogo, and lemon per the instructions in the ingredients list. Mix all the ingredients for the salsa.

Place the 'opihi on the grill, shell-side down. Cook until juices start to bubble out from under the edges of the shells. Remove the limpets from the heat and arrange, meat-side up, on a serving platter. Top with the salsa and serve with lemon wedges on the side.

Yield: 4 servings

24 large 'opihi (legal size!)
Kiawe charcoal, for grilling
½ lemon, cut into wedges (for garnish)

For the salsa:

1 small Kula onion, cut into ⅛-inch dice
2 stalks green onion, sliced fine
1 medium-sized ripe tomato, seeded and cut into ⅛-inch dice
½ cup chopped ogo seaweed
3 tablespoons soy sauce
2 tablespoons chili pepper water (see recipe below)

Kula Onion Chili Pepper Water

Chili pepper water is an Island tradition and the perfect way to add some pizzazz to your food. This Maui version of the staple is spiced with onion, garlic, ginger, and sugar, and adds more flavor than just plain HOT. You'll be tempted to dip your chopsticks in the bottle and munch on some of the onion and ginger.

Remove the chili pepper stems; cut the peppers in half. Careful not to touch your fingers to your mouth or eyes; the juices will burn you. Put the chili peppers in the glass bottle.

Cut up the onion, garlic, and ginger per the instructions in the ingredients list, and add to the bottle with the vinegar, sugar, and Hawaiian salt.

Bring the water to a boil and pour it into the jar, over all the chopped vegetables. Put the lid or cap on the jar and let it cool. When it is cool, put it in the refrigerator and let it marinate overnight. You can keep it in your refrigerator up to a month. It gets better by the day.

Yield: 2½ to 3 cups

10 Hawaiian chili peppers, stems removed
½ cup Kula onion, peeled and thinly sliced
3 cloves garlic, peeled and thinly sliced
1 (1-inch long) thumb of fresh ginger, peeled and thinly sliced
2 cups boiling water
2 tablespoons Hawaiian salt
2 tablespoons white vinegar
1 teaspoon sugar
1 (3-cup) glass bottle with lid or cap

Spicy White Crab Poke

Yield: 10 to 12 servings

3 pounds white (kuahonu) crab, fresh or frozen

For the marinade:

½ cup finely minced Kula onion

4 stalks green onion, thinly sliced

3 cloves garlic, finely minced

1 teaspoon chili pepper flakes

½ teaspoon cayenne pepper

½ teaspoon paprika

6 tablespoons sesame oil

1 tablespoon honey

*C*rabbing is a favorite Island outing, and one that can be enjoyed by all ages. Get the 'ohana together to catch sweet white crabs just off Maui's famous Sugar Beach. All you need to do is bait a crab net, stand in the shallows, and throw the net. Every 10 or 15 minutes, pull in the net to see if you've caught any crabs.

Of course, it's more complicated than that … you can get an experienced crabber to show you the tricks. It's not that hard, and you'll have a bucket full of crabs in no time.

When you've got them, try this tasty poke.

If you are working with fresh live crabs it is best to put them in a plastic bag and leave them in the freezer for 20 to 30 minutes. This should make handling them easier for the cleaning process.

Remove the top shell and discard. Remove the gills and rinse the crab under cold running water. Cut the body in quarters with a sharp knife and refrigerate the crab pieces while preparing the marinade.

If you purchased frozen raw crab that is available in the fish markets, it will most likely be cleaned and ready to use.

Prepare the onion, green onion, and garlic per the instructions in the ingredients list. Mix all the ingredients for the marinade. Put the chunks of crab meat in a dish with a cover; pour the marinade over the crab. Toss the crab to make sure that every chunk is coated with marinade. Cover and chill overnight.

PRESENTATION

Serve this spicy raw crab poke chilled with lots of old newspaper laid out on the tables for your empty shells.

Shoyu Hagi

Yield: 4 servings

4 whole hagi (black triggerfish) about 1½ pounds each. This will give you about 6 pounds.
1 clove garlic, put through a garlic press
1 (thumb-sized) piece of ginger, peeled and grated
Salt and pepper to taste
2 tablespoons cooking oil
1 cup soy sauce
1 cup water
1 cup brown sugar
1 tablespoon sesame oil
1 stalk green onion, finely chopped (for garnish)

(Courtesy of John Keanaaina)

"*My dad loved to fish for hagi, or black triggerfish. After a hard day at work, he could sit and fish for a couple of hours; he usually caught enough hagi to make a delicious meal for everyone. Hagi are a great fish to serve to keiki, because they have only a few, large bones. Keiki still learning to eat fish can enjoy hagi. This fish is easy to catch and found everywhere in Hawaiian waters. It makes great poke and is delicious fried. Sometimes, it can be found at open markets, rarely at fish counters.*"

Skin and clean the hagi.

Prepare the garlic and ginger per the instructions in the ingredients list. Season the hagi fillets with salt and pepper to taste.

Pour the 2 tablespoons of cooking oil into the bottom of a large pot over medium-high heat. When the oil is hot, add the hagi fillets. Brown on both sides.

Add the garlic, ginger, soy sauce, water, sugar, and sesame oil to the pot and turn the heat up to high. Bring the fish to a boil and then reduce the heat until the fish is just barely simmering. Cook for 35 minutes.

While the fish is simmering, you can cut up the green onion for the garnish.

PRESENTATION

John likes to present the fish in a deep serving dish, garnished with green onions.

He often pairs this dish with fresh rice and sautéed 'uala, or sweet potato leaves. He adds some garlic butter and dried shrimp, 'ōpae, to the leaves. 'Ono!

Sautéed Kūpe'e

(Courtesy of John Keanaaina)

Yield: 2 servings

2 cups kūpe'e
2 cloves minced garlic
2 tablespoons butter

"The kūpe'e is a nocturnal sea snail that is three to four times larger than the diurnal (daytime) snails, the pipipi. It lives on rocky ocean floors with coarse sand. Kūpe'e are usually harvested at night, when the tide is low. When my 'ohana and I went out at night to get 'a'ama, or black crab, we would collect kūpe'e as well."

Because kūpe'e vary so much in size, and the catch will vary from day to day, it's impossible to give fixed amounts for the snails, garlic, and butter. You'll want to use enough butter to keep the snails and garlic from burning; use the garlic to season the snails to your taste. Experiment and enjoy!

Wash the kūpe'e under running water in a colander and drain them well.

Mince the garlic and melt the butter in a sauté pan over medium heat. Add the garlic and kūpe'e. Cook for 5 minutes, stirring frequently.

PRESENTATION

Kūpe'e are served in the shell; diners use a snail pick or a bamboo skewer to pull out the tasty meat. John likes to serve them with baked taro.

Steamed Manila Clams

*F*resh clams cooked in a savory stock, with local corn and Portuguese sausage—yum!

Scrub the clams well with a stiff brush. Discard any clams that don't shut when you handle them; these are dead. Dissolve 1 tablespoon salt in a gallon of water and add the clams. Let them soak for 20 minutes; rinse and put in fresh salt water. Repeat two more times and drain.

Cut up the green onions, garlic, corn, sausage, and watercress according to the instructions in the ingredients list.

Heat the olive oil in a large pot over medium-high heat. When the oil is hot, add the sausage, garlic, chili flakes, and clams. Sauté for 2 minutes. Add the white wine, corn, and chicken stock and continue cooking until all the clams have opened. Add the chopped green onions and watercress. Add the butter and season with salt and pepper to taste. Serve immediately.

Yield: 2 to 4 servings

2 pounds live Manila clams
4 stalks green onions, thinly sliced
2 teaspoons garlic, chopped
2 ears fresh Kula corn, cut across the cob into 1½ inch rounds
½ cup diced chorizo or Portuguese sausage (½-inch dice)
1 cup chopped fresh watercress (cut in 2-inch pieces)
1 tablespoon olive oil
¼ teaspoon dried chili pepper flakes
½ cup white wine
2 cups chicken stock
1 tablespoon butter
Salt and pepper to taste

Black and Blue Aku

Yield: 4 to 6 servings

¼ cup diced Kula onion
(¼-inch dice)

2 tablespoons chopped
green onion

¼ cup seeded and diced
Roma tomato (¼-inch
dice)

¼ cup seeded and diced
Japanese cucumber
(¼-inch dice)

1 pound aku fillets

1 teaspoon sea salt

1 tablespoon Volcano Spice
Mild Cajun Blend
OR your favorite Cajun
spice for seafood

2 tablespoons vegetable oil

1½ tablespoons soy sauce

2 teaspoons sesame oil

2 teaspoons sambal oelek
(Indonesian chili paste)

Aku, or skipjack tuna, is an affordable alternative to 'ahi. It has robust flavor that is nicely complemented by the assertive spices in this tasty fish salad. I like to use the Mild Cajun Blend from our local spice company, Volcano Spice Seasonings. Of course, you can substitute your favorite Cajun blend if you prefer. As for the aku—if you're lucky, you will find fishermen selling their fresh catch at Kahului harbor. Look for Fresh Aku signs propped against cars on the side of the road.

Cut up the onion, green onion, tomato, and cucumber per the instructions in the ingredients list.

Rub the aku fillets with sea salt and Volcano Spice. Put the oil in a sauté pan over high heat. When the oil is hot (close to smoking) quickly sear the outside of the fillets. The fish should remain rare in the center. Remove the aku from the heat, put in a covered container, and refrigerate until completely cool.

While the aku is cooling, mix all the cut vegetables, the soy sauce, sesame oil, and sambal oelek in a serving bowl.

Cut the cooled aku into 1-inch cubes and add them to the bowl. Using two spoons, gently toss everything together. Serve cold.

Maui Kine Grindz

This chapter is about more than just plate-lunch food. It's about comfort food—the food that you buy at your local drive-in, at the county fair, or take to potlucks as a special treat. It's the food you crave when you're off-island: chow fun, teri beef, chili, tripe stew, ribs pipikaula-style, and so on. It's the food that locals grew up with and visitors quickly learn to love—the food that says "home." Of course you can get many of these dishes on the other islands too, but they taste so much better when they're made with Maui ingredients, by Maui chefs.

Whether you're a local now living on the mainland, or you're still right here on Maui, the Hamburger Steak with Kula Onion Gravy, the Poi Waffle Dogs, and Char Siu Pork Ribs will fill your kitchen with the smells of good old-fashioned Maui cooking.

We eat to make us feel good,
We eat 'cuz someone made it,
We eat 'cuz we crave it!

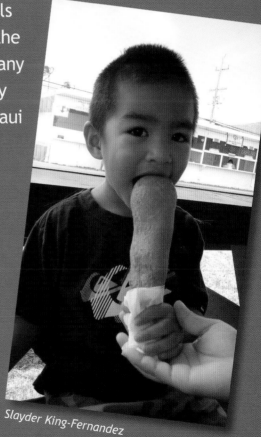

Slayder King-Fernandez

Dry Mein

*S*am Sato's restaurant in the Wailuku industrial area is famous for its freshly baked, hand-made manju (a bean paste-filled bun) and for its wonderful dry mein noodles. Here's my version of their popular noodle dish that comes close to the real thing. Can't promise that it will have the real Sam Sato taste but it should satisfy your noodle cravings without the long wait in line.

Yield: 4 to 5 servings

½ pound char siu
¼ cup finely sliced green onions
1 pound fresh saimin noodles
3 tablespoons vegetable oil
5 ounces (½ package) bean sprouts
2 tablespoons soy sauce
½ teaspoon salt or to taste
¼ teaspoon black pepper or to taste

Cut the char siu into slivers ⅛-inch wide and 1½ inches long. Clean, trim, and slice the green onions.

Bring 2 quarts water to a boil. Add the saimin and cook, at a simmer, until the noodles are done. This should take about 2 minutes. Pour the cooked noodles into a colander and cool under running water. Drain well.

Heat the oil in a frying pan over medium-high heat. Add the slivers of char siu, the bean sprouts, and noodles. Cook, stirring, until all ingredients are heated and the bean sprouts have wilted. Add the soy sauce, salt, and pepper and mix well. Top with the sliced green onions and serve hot.

'Ono BBQ Chicken

Yield: 6 to 8 servings

3 pounds boneless, skinless chicken thighs

For the marinade:
¼ cup finely sliced green onions
2 tablespoons minced garlic
1 tablespoon peeled and minced ginger
1 cup soy sauce
1 cup light brown sugar
1 cup water
½ cup mirin
2 tablespoons sesame oil
¼ to ½ tablespoon dried chili pepper flakes (more if you like it hot)

1 tablespoon toasted sesame seeds, for the garnish

This is my version of barbeque chicken. Whenever the family and I take this chicken dish to potlucks, only the empty pan comes home. Bring this to the next potluck you attend and you will know why it's called 'ono BBQ chicken.

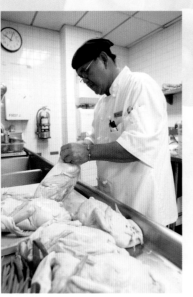

Prepare the green onions, garlic, and ginger per the ingredients list for the marinade. Put all the marinade ingredients in a large container with a lid and mix well. Add the boneless chicken thighs to the marinade; cover and leave in the refrigerator overnight. Turn or stir occasionally for even marination.

Grill chicken over a moderate kiawe charcoal fire until both sides are done. If you don't have a grill, you can cook the chicken under your oven broiler. Arrange on a platter or individual plates, and garnish with a sprinkle of sesame seeds.

Teri-Miso Butterfish

*T*eriyaki dishes are marinated in teriyaki sauce and broiled or grilled; misoyaki dishes are marinated in a miso marinade and broiled or grilled. Someone, somewhere, decided to combine the two kinds of marinade. The classic Japanese version is marinaded in miso then glazed with teriyaki sauce. My version combines both flavors. The result is simply delicious. I consider this teri-miso butterfish one of da best Maui grindz.

Peel and grate the ginger. Combine all marinade ingredients in a medium bowl and whisk together until the sugar and miso have completely dissolved. There should be no sugar grit or miso lumps.

Pour the marinade into a large resealable zip-lock plastic bag; add the butterfish fillets, and seal the bag. Put the bag in the refrigerator and let the fish marinate overnight. Turn a few times to ensure even marination.

The next day, turn your broiler to high. Arrange the drained fillets on a rack in a broiler pan. Broil 6 to 8 minutes on each side. Be careful not to burn. Serve immediately.

Yield: 4 to 6 servings

2 pounds butterfish fillets

For the marinade:
2 teaspoons fresh ginger, peeled and grated
½ cup soy sauce
½ cup sugar
½ cup miso
¼ cup mirin

Tonkatsu (Pork Cutlet)

Yield: 4 servings

4 slices (4 ounces each) boneless pork loin
½ teaspoon salt
¼ teaspoon pepper
½ cup flour
2 eggs, beaten
1 cup panko (Japanese-style bread crumbs)
4 tablespoons vegetable oil for frying
1 cup shredded napa cabbage

For the tonkatsu sauce:
(Makes ½ cup sauce)
2 tablespoons peeled and grated ginger
½ cup ketchup
¼ cup sugar
2 tablespoons Worcestershire sauce
½ teaspoon Coleman's mustard powder

My way! My version of tonkatsu sauce. This sauce can also be used with chicken.

To prepare the sauce, peel and grate the ginger. Combine all ingredients in a small saucepan and bring to a boil over medium-high heat. Simmer for 2 minutes. Cool before serving.

Season the pork slices with the salt and pepper. Dredge the pork slices in flour and dip in the beaten egg. Let excess egg drip off. Put the slices in a pan of panko and coat evenly.

Heat vegetable oil in a frying pan over medium high heat. Fry the pork cutlets on both sides until they are crisp and golden brown. Drain on a paper towel. Before serving, slice the cutlets into strips and arrange on shredded napa cabbage. Serve with tonkatsu sauce.

Maui County Fair

There are a handful of events people look forward to all year: birthdays, Christmas, New Year's, the first day of summer vacation. Most Maui people would also include the Maui County Fair. On the last weekend of September, everyone heads down to the Maui's War Memorial Complex for rides, entertainment, and plenty of 'ono fair food—teri beef, malassadas, and the Boy Scouts' signature Pronto Pups. But the fair isn't just about the food and the rides. There are also games and exhibits and contests where Maui farmers, ranchers, craftspeople, and gardeners can show off their products. There's no better way to say goodbye to summer than with a two-pound plate of food and a pocketful of scrip.

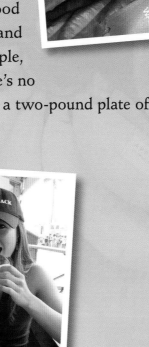

Udon

Yield: 4 servings

2 (10.5-ounce) packages
fresh or fresh-frozen
udon

For the broth:
8 cups water
½ cup usukushi soy sauce
3 tablespoons mirin
2 tablespoons sake
1¾ teaspoon hondashi

For the garnish:
2 hard boiled eggs, cut in
half
4 teaspoons finely sliced
green onions
2 ounces kamaboko fish
cake, approximately 8
slices
4 teaspoons dry wakame
seaweed, soaked,
drained, and chopped
8 pieces cooked (16/20)
shrimp

*M*aui folks enjoy many tasty Japanese dishes, like sushi, musubi, teriyaki, and udon. Udon are thick wheat noodles, often served in soup. Maui's many Japanese visitors also love their udon, and udon soup and fried udon are found on many hotel and restaurant menus.

The udon is best cooked in a large metal strainer. You can dip the noodles in boiling water, hold them there for a few minutes, and lift them out easily. You can buy noodle strainers in cooking supply stores or some Japanese groceries. When it's cold up in Kula, there's nothing like a bowl of hot soup full of noodles with tasty garnishes.

Prepare the garnishes per the ingredients list. Boil, cool, peel, and cut up the eggs; slice the green onions; cut the kamaboko into ¼-inch thick slices; soak, drain, and chop the wakame; quickly boil the shrimp if you have purchased raw shrimp. (Cook in boiling water for 2 to 3 minutes, turn off the heat, and let the shrimp sit for 15 minutes or so. Peel and remove the dark vein down the back.)

Measure 8 cups of water into a large pot and bring to a boil. Add the soy sauce, mirin, sake and hondashi. Turn the heat down and let the soup simmer while you prepare the udon.

Boil water in another pot. Put the udon in a large strainer and dip it into the pot of boiling water. Let the noodles cook for 2 minutes; remove and drain well.

Divide the noodles evenly between 4 large bowls. Divide all the garnishes evenly between the bowls. Add hot broth to cover and serve immediately.

Chopsteak with Maui Onion

Yield: 6 to 8 servings

2 pounds beef flap steak
   (flap meat)
1 large Maui onion

For the marinade:
2 tablespoons soy sauce
2 teaspoons sake
2 teaspoons sugar
4 teaspoons cornstarch
2 teaspoons kosher salt or
   to taste
½ teaspoon coarse-grind
   black pepper or to taste
2 tablespoons vegetable oil
   for stir-frying

This is comfort food for local people. We served this at the Maui Country Fair to raise money for Baldwin High School Project Graduation and it disappeared quickly.

Cut the flap steak into ¼-inch slices and then into strips 2 inches long. Cut the onion in half and then into ¼-inch slices.

Mix the soy sauce, sake, sugar, cornstarch, salt, and pepper in a container with a cover that is large enough to hold the sliced beef. Add the sliced beef and mix well. Let the beef marinate for 20 minutes, covered in refrigerator.

Heat 1 tablespoon of vegetable oil in a wok over medium high heat. Brown the onions, stirring frequently; don't let them burn. Remove them from the wok and set aside.

Turn the heat under the wok up to high. Add 1 tablespoon of vegetable oil and stir-fry the beef strips, stirring constantly. They should be nicely browned but not burnt. Add the cooked onions at the last minute and toss the steak and onions together before turning off the heat and serving the steak.

Sweet-Sour Spare Ribs

*F*or twenty years, Richard Kimura has been serving these 'ono ribs at the Maui County Fair. His booth raises money for the King's Cathedral Music Ministry. Great cause, great ribs. The ribs are cooked in a broth flavored with ginger and star anise. Star anise is a small, star-shaped brown fruit widely used in East Asian and South Asian cooking.

Cut up the meat per the ingredients list. Fill two large pots with water. Put the ribs in one, the pork cubes in another. Bring both pots to a boil, then reduce the heat and simmer the meat for approximately 45 to 55 minutes, or until the meat is tender. Skim off any impurities that float to the surface of the water. Remove the meat and drain.

Peel and thinly slice the ginger for the sauce. Mix the water, soy sauce, sugar, and vinegar in a large pot, add the ginger and star anise, and bring the mixture to a boil. Turn down the heat and simmer for 30 minutes. Scoop out the ginger and star anise out of the sauce before thickening with a strainer. Mix the cornstarch and water until you have a uniform paste. Stir the cornstarch slurry into the sauce and simmer, stirring for several minutes while the sauce thickens.

Add the cubes of boiled meat to the sauce and simmer for another 30 minutes. Just before serving, stir in the five-spice powder; this adds extra taste and aroma to an already delightful dish.

Yield: 20 to 25 servings

5 pounds pork spare ribs, cut into 1½-inch cubes
5 pounds boneless pork butt, cut into 1½-inch cubes
¼ teaspoon five-spice powder (added at the very end)

For the sauce:
¼ cup ginger peeled and sliced thin
1½ cups water
1½ cups Kikkoman soy sauce
1½ cups apple cider vinegar
4 to 5 pieces whole star anise
1½ cups brown turbinado sugar (Maui raw sugar)

For the cornstarch slurry:
4 tablespoons cornstarch
½ cup cold water

Poi Waffle Dogs

*Y*es, these are the famous poi waffle dogs sold at Baldwin High School basketball games. More fun than the action on the court! You'll need a waffle iron to make them.

Thread the wooden popsicle sticks through the hot dogs, the long way.

Sift together the flour, sugar, baking powder, and salt. Mix the poi, eggs, milk, and oil. Add the liquids to the sifted ingredient in three increments, beating after each addition. Don't overbeat; it's OK if there are a few small lumps.

Heat the waffle iron and lightly spray the plates with cooking spray, to prevent sticking. Pour poi batter onto the bottom plate and put one hot dog, on its stick, into the center of the waffle. Close the iron and cook until the waffle is crisp and lightly browned. Serve hot with mustard and ketchup.

Yield: 8 servings

8 Maui hot dogs
8 wooden popsicle sticks

For the batter:
1¼ cup all-purpose flour
2 tablespoon sugar
4 teaspoons baking powder
¾ teaspoon salt
½ cup poi
2 whole eggs, beaten
1 cup milk
4 tablespoons vegetable oil

Cooking spray for cooking the waffle dogs

Pronto Pup

*T*his Maui Grindz is one that you crave for all year long until the Maui County fair is back in town. Its has been The Maui County Council, Boy Scouts of America annual fund raising booth for over 30 years where hundreds of these tasty treats are sold. Eddie Tamanaha long time Boy Scout enthusiast from Troop 68 in Wailuku has the pronto pup dip, twist and drop down to a science. Cooking the prefect pronto pup is not as easy as he makes it look. Believe me I spent a few shifts in the booth during my Cub Master days.

Skewer hot dogs with the wooden sticks. Mix the egg, water, and evaporated milk in a bowl. Next add the rest of the ingredients, mixing until the batter is smooth. Heat oil for deep-frying to 350 degrees. Dip each hot dog into the batter then into the oil. Fry until golden brown and serve.

Yield: 10 each

10 each hot dogs, all beef
10 each wooden stir or popsicle sticks
Oil for deep-frying

For the batter:
1 whole egg, beaten
1 cup water
2 tablespoons evaporated milk
3 tablespoons sugar
½ cup flour
2 cups Bisquick

Maui Cattle Company Teriyaki Beef Rib-Eye

Yield: 4 servings

2 pounds Maui Cattle Co.
rib-eye steak, cut into
¼-inch slices

½ cup flour for dredging
meat

4 tablespoons vegetable oil
for sautéing

For the marinade:

1 teaspoon peeled and
grated ginger

2 medium cloves garlic,
minced

¾ cup soy sauce

½ cup water

¼ cup sugar

Cupies Drive-In in Kahului is a favorite spot for great Maui grindz. Their breaded teriyaki beef is one of their most popular items. Now you can make it at home—and it's quick and easy too! For the full Cupies experience, enjoy your teri beef with freshly-cooked white rice and some mac salad. They make it for take out.

Peel and grate the ginger; mince the garlic. Combine all the marinade ingredients in a bowl and mix well. Add the sliced rib-eye steak. Marinate the steak for 2 hours in covered container and refrigerate. Turn or stir occasionally for even marination.

Sprinkle flour into a shallow pan. Remove the meat from the marinade and dredge the slices in flour. Shake off any excess flour.

Heat a frying pan over medium-high heat. Add some vegetable oil to lightly coat the pan and sauté the beef until nicely browned; this should take about 1½ to 2 minutes on each side. Serve immediately.

County Fair Chow Fun

Yield: 6 to 7 servings

1 cup Kula onion, sliced ⅛-inch wide and 1½ inch long

½ cup carrots, sliced ⅛-inch wide and 1½ inch long

½ cup celery, sliced ⅛-inch wide and 1½ inch long

1 tablespoon peeled and minced ginger

4 stalks green onions, sliced fine for garnish

2 tablespoons vegetable oil

1 pound ground pork

2 pounds fresh chow fun noodles

2 tablespoons oyster sauce

1 tablespoon soy sauce

1 teaspoon salt or to taste

½ teaspoon pepper or to taste

1 (10-ounce) package bean sprouts

This tasty noodle dish makes an annual appearance at the Maui County Fair, where hundreds of portions are served by Wailuku Hongwanji Mission. It's served in paper cones lined up in custom-made holders, ready to be filled. The cones are consumed by hungry fair-goers as fast as they are finished. Now you don't have to wait until fair-time to enjoy this version of county fair chow fun.

Chow fun noodles are wide rice noodles. Buy them fresh and use them immediately; they will dry out quickly. They do not need to be boiled before they are stir-fried. If you boil them, they will turn to mush. You really need a HOT wok and constant stirring to keep them from turning into a mushy mess. A regular frying pan won't do the job.

Prepare the onion, carrot, celery, ginger, and green onion per the directions in the ingredient list.

Heat the vegetable oil in a wok over medium-high heat. It should be sizzling hot, but not smoking. Add the ground pork and minced ginger and brown the pork, breaking it into bits with the wok spatula and stirring it constantly.

Add the onions, carrots, and celery and continue frying and stirring. Keep the heat up and the spatula moving. When the vegetables have wilted, season with the oyster sauce, soy sauce, salt, and pepper.

Add the chow fun noodles and toss until they are thoroughly warm and coated with sauce. Stir in the bean sprouts and green onions and turn off the heat. The hot chow fun will cook them in no time. When they have wilted, dish up the chow fun.

Macaroni Salad

*M*ac salad is an Island staple; everyone has his or her own version. My version is fully loaded; still, it's simple but tasty. You can make this recipe fancier by substituting crab meat for the tuna and/or adding a cup of cooked green peas. Experiment! Have fun!

Hard-boil the eggs. They will be easier to shell if you run cold water over them when you take them out of the water.

Bring a large pot of salted water to boil and add the macaroni. Stir so that the macaroni doesn't clump. Boil the macaroni until al dente. Drain in a colander; run water over macaroni to cool it quickly.

Drain the tuna. Peel and coarsely grate the hardboiled eggs. Peel and grate the carrots. Mix the macaroni, tuna, eggs, carrots, celery, and mayonnaise. Add the salt and pepper; taste and correct the seasoning if necessary. Chill before serving.

Yield: 6 to 8 servings

6 hardboiled eggs
1 pound elbow macaroni
1 can tuna (7 ounces),
    packed in water
¼ cup finely grated carrots
¼ cup minced celery
2 cups mayonnaise
1 tablespoon kosher salt or
    to taste
¼ tablespoon white pepper
    or to taste

Char Siu Pork Ribs

*S*aint Louis-style pork ribs are a specialty cut of spare ribs where the brisket bones are removed. If you don't see them at the meat counter or the butcher shop, ask to have them prepared for you.

Yield: 8 to 10 servings

6 pounds Saint Louis-style pork ribs

For the rub:
1¼ pound sugar
3 tablespoons salt
½ tablespoon white pepper
½ tablespoon Chinese five-spice powder
1 tablespoon red bean curd
1 tablespoon hoisin sauce
Red food coloring (optional)

¼ cup honey to glaze

Mix all the ingredients for the rub. Add red coloring if desired. Cover the pork ribs generously with the rub and put them in a steel or glass covered container. Let them marinate in the refrigerator for 3 days; turn periodically so that they marinate evenly.

Preheat the oven to 450 degrees. Place the ribs on a rack in a foil-lined pan. Cook the ribs at 450 degrees for 20 minutes, then turn the heat down to 350 degrees. Cook for another 15 to 20 minutes. Check the interior of the ribs with a meat thermometer; the thermometer should register 160 degrees. If the pork hasn't reached that temperature, cook for a few more minutes and test again. It's good to be safe with pork.

When the ribs are done (cooked to 160 degrees), remove them from the oven and brush them with the honey. Let the ribs rest for 10 minutes. Slice between the rib bones and serve.

Chef Ribucan's Award-Winning Maui Chili

Yield: 14 to 16 servings

2½ pounds cubed Maui Cattle Co. boneless chuck, cut in ½ inch cubes

4 cups sweet Maui onions, finely diced (about 2 whole Maui onions)

1 (28-ounce) can crushed tomatoes

4 medium cloves garlic, put through a press

1 tablespoons finely chopped fresh basil

1 tablespoons olive oil

2 bay leaves

2 beef bouillon cube

2½ tablespoons chili powder

2½ tablespoons ground cumin

2 teaspoons cayenne pepper

1 tablespoons brown sugar

½ tablespoon black pepper or to taste

2 teaspoons Hawaiian salt or to taste

*C*hef Sean Ribucan, who works with me, is the two-time winner of the Maui regional chili cook-off. This is his award-winning recipe. Maui Cattle Co. natural free-range, lean and flavorful beef chuck works well for this recipe.

Chili aficionados argue about whether or not chili should have beans. This recipe calls for an all-meat chili, but if you like beans in your chili, you can add a #10 can (about 16 cups) of cooked kidney beans or add beans that you've cooked yourself.

If you're going to eat this dish Maui-style, serve over freshly-cooked rice, with mayonnaise and hot sauce on the side. You can use Tabasco sauce or homemade chili pepper water.

Trim the beef and cut it into ½-inch cubes. Peel and dice the onions. Open the can of tomatoes. Peel the garlic and put it through a garlic press; wash and chop the basil.

Heat the olive oil in a large stockpot over medium-high heat. Brown the meat in the oil. Reduce the heat to medium, add the onions and garlic, and sweat them. That means to cook them without browning. Add the tomatoes and the bay leaves, bouillon cubes, chili powder, ground cumin, cayenne pepper, brown sugar, black pepper, and salt. Don't add the basil; you're saving that for the end.

Lower the heat under the pot to medium and simmer the stew until the flavors have mingled and the cubes of meat (if you have used cubes rather than ground beef) are tender. Stir frequently; this stew is thick and burns easily. This step should take about 45 minutes.

About 5 minutes before you plan to serve the chili, turn off the heat and add the chopped basil. Let the chili sit for 5 minutes, then taste. Adjust the seasoning, adding more salt, pepper, cayenne pepper, or sugar, as necessary.

Portuguese Bean Soup

(Courtesy of Larry Rocha)

Yield: 8 to 10 servings

*L*arry Rocha is known for his "GPS", or Good Portuguese Soup. He dishes up big bowls of GPS at the Maui County Fair, at the Maui Veterans booth. It's a great soup; you can taste the aloha in every spoonful. He was kind enough to share his recipe.

Fill a large soup pot with 3 quarts of water and start it heating over medium-high heat. Rinse the kidney beans and chop the Portuguese sausage and the onion per the instructions in the ingredients list. Add the ham hock, Portuguese sausage, kidney beans, chopped onion, and tomato sauce to the pot. Bring the soup to a boil, then turn the heat down and simmer the soup on low for 1½ hours, or until the ham falls off the hock bones. Stir occasionally, and add extra water as needed to keep the soup from burning.

While the soup is cooking, cut up the potatoes, carrots, and watercress per the ingredients list.

Remove the sausage and ham hock from the soup. Cut the meat off the ham hocks and chop it into small pieces, discarding the rest of the hock. Set the sausage and ham chunks aside.

Add the chopped potatoes and carrots to the soup and simmer them until they are tender, about 20 minutes. Put the cut-up sausage and ham back into the soup, together with the cut-up watercress. Turn off the heat under the pot. Taste the soup; add a dash of soy sauce and taste again. Correct the seasoning if necessary.

PRESENTATION
Traditionally served with one scoop rice.

Ingredients

- 3 quarts water
- 2 (16-ounce packages) dried red kidney beans, washed
- 2 ham hocks
- 2 (12-ounce) Portuguese sausages (Larry likes the Ah Fook brand)
- 1 medium-sized round onion, roughly chopped
- 3 (5-ounce) cans tomato sauce
- 3 medium-sized potatoes, peeled and cut into 1-inch dice
- 4 medium-sized carrots, peeled and cut into 1-inch dice
- 1 (16-ounce) bunch watercress, cut into 3-inch lengths
- Soy sauce to taste (Larry likes the Aloha brand)
- Salt and pepper to taste

Lechon Kawali

Yield: 6 to 8 servings

5 pounds pork belly with
 the rind on
1 quart water
3 garlic cloves, peeled and
 crushed
1 bay leaf
2 tablespoons cider vinegar
2 tablespoons Hawaiian salt
 or to taste
¼ teaspoon ground black
 pepper or to taste

Oil for deep frying

For the dipping sauce:
1 clove garlic, minced
1 shallot, minced
1 small Hawaiian chili
 pepper, trimmed,
 deseeded, and minced
3 tablespoons soy sauce
5 tablespoons vinegar

Alex Caoile owns Family Restaurant and Catering in Kahului. We used to work together at the Westin Maui Resort. His restaurant is famous for the comfort food it serves and Lechon Kawali is a favorite Filipino one. In the Philippines, lechon restaurants are everywhere. The acronym AFRO is for Adobo Fried Rice Omelette.

Cut the pork belly into 1-inch cubes. Fill a large stockpot with 1 quart water. Add the pork cubes, garlic, bay leaf, vinegar, salt, and pepper. Bring to a boil over high heat; turn down the heat and simmer for 1 hour and 25 minutes. Remove the boiled pork to a colander and rinse well under cold water; drain. Put the pork in the refrigerator covered, to chill before you fry it.

While the pork is chilling, you can make the dipping sauce. Peel and mince the garlic and shallot; add the chili pepper. Combine all the sauce ingredients in a small bowl and set aside.

Heat oil in a fryer or deep pot to 350 degrees. Deep-fry the pork cubes until brown and crisp. You will probably need to do this in several batches; do not crowd the oil. Drain the pork cubes on paper towels before serving with dipping sauce.

Shoyu Short Ribs Pipikaula-Style

Yield: 6 to 8 servings

Upcountry Maui has been cattle country since the early 1800s, when cattle first came to the islands and Hawaiian cowboys or paniolos, learned to ride, rope, and herd. Lacking refrigerators, early ranchers preserved beef by sundrying it and turning it into jerky. Hawaiian-kine jerky is called pipikaula, or beef string. It's usually spicier and softer than mainland jerky.

This innovative short rib recipe treats the ribs pipikaula style. The ribs are marinated and then slowly oven dried. Store them in the refrigerator and briefly fry or broil before eating.

Cut the short ribs into individual ribs and then cut each rib into chunks ¾-inch long. Prepare the ginger and garlic per the instructions in the ingredients list.

Mix all the marinade ingredients in a large container with a lid. Add the short ribs. Cover and refrigerate for 2 hours. Turn the rib chunks frequently, so that they marinate evenly.

Preheat the oven to 165 degrees. Remove the ribs from the container, letting any excess marinade drain off. Set them on a wire rack in a foil-lined broiler pan or baking pan. The sliced ribs should be well-separated; if they touch, they will not dry evenly. Dry the meat in the preheated oven for 3 hours. Turn the ribs over and dry for another 3 hours.

Remove the ribs from the oven and let them cool completely. Wrap them well and store them in your refrigerator. They will keep for 2 weeks.

Before serving, pan-fry the short ribs in a little vegetable oil over medium-high heat, until they are brown on both sides. You can also broil them over a kiawe charcoal fire.

Ingredients:

4 pounds short ribs, sliced ¾-inch thick

For the marinade:
2 teaspoons ginger peeled and grated
1 teaspoon minced garlic
½ teaspoon crushed dried red chili peppers, or to taste
1 cup soy sauce
½ cup sugar
¼ cup mirin

Hamburger Steak with Kula Onion Gravy

Yield: 6 to 8 servings

1 cup finely chopped sweet
    Kula onion
1 tablespoon minced garlic
1 tablespoon chopped
    parsley
2 eggs, beaten
2 pounds Maui Cattle Co.
    ground beef chuck
½ cup panko (Japanese
    bread crumbs)
½ cup milk
2 tablespoons garlic
    peppercorn ketchup
    (Tedeschi Winery bottles
    this, right on Maui)
2 teaspoons Worcestershire
    sauce
2 teaspoons kosher salt or
    to taste
1 teaspoon ground black
    pepper or to taste
Oil for frying

2 cups Kula Onion Gravy
    (see recipe on page 127)
    (optional)

*T*his hamburger steak becomes extraordinary when made with free-range Maui beef and the famous Kula sweet onions. It's your classic hamburger steak.

If you're serving this with Kula onion gravy, make up the gravy before you start frying the meat.

Chop the onion, garlic, and parsley, and beat the eggs. Mix all ingredients. Divide into 6 to 8 equal-sized patties and shape the patties with your hands.

Heat a slick of vegetable oil in a frying pan over medium-high heat. Fry the patties in vegetable oil until golden brown on each side and cooked through. Serve topped with Kula onion gravy.

Kula Onion Gravy

*K*ula Onions come from Bryan Otani Farms. When the onions caramelize, they give a distinct flavor to the sauce. A good pairing with the Maui Cattle Company's beef. All from Upcountry.

Peel and chop the onions.

Melt the butter in a large saucepan over medium heat. Add the chopped onions and sauté them, stirring occasionally, until they are caramelized (soft, brown, and sweet). Don't let them burn. This may take up to 30 minutes.

Add the flour to the caramelized onions and stir. The flour should form a brown paste, a roux. Add the beef broth gradually, stirring continuously. The butter-soaked flour will swell, thickening the gravy. If you don't stir, the gravy may lump.

When the gravy has thickened, turn down the heat under the pan and simmer the gravy for another 10 minutes, stirring occasionally.

Yield: 4 cups

2 cups coarsely chopped
  Kula onion
4 tablespoons butter
4 tablespoons flour
4 cups beef broth
Salt and pepper to taste

Guest Chefs

O ver the years, I've been lucky to make friends with other Maui chefs who share my passion for Island culture and locally grown, sustainable ingredients. My friends are so talented, and always willing to experiment. Thanks to their efforts, Maui is developing its own world-class cuisine.

My colleagues are generous too; they shared some of their best recipes with me. And now I'd like to share them with you. Some of the dishes are simple, like charred pineapple or moi poke; others, like Bev Gannon's goat cheese-stuffed chicken breasts, may require a bit more practice. But, whether it's slow-cooked Korean kalbi or fresh and cool Mango Gazpacho, you're sure to find something that'll impress everyone at your next potluck or party.

Beef Shank Laulau

Chef Perry Bateman, Mama's Fish House, Pā'ia

"**B**eing Hawaiian, the love of Hawaiian food is in my koko. One of my favorite dishes is laulau. Laulau is a leaf bundle in which we bake pork, beef, chicken, or butterfish, together with ulu (breadfruit), sweet potato, or kalo (taro). We use ti and kalo leaves for wrapping. The traditional way to make laulau is to bake them in an imu (earth oven). These days, imu are only for special occasions, The rest of the time, we make the laulau in a steamer or a pressure cooker. We lose the lovely smoky imu taste, but the laulau are still 'ono.*

I experimented until I figured out a way to make the best beef laulau ever. Secret? Beef shank, which is full of flavor but low in fat, AND thin slices of fat from a beef roast. You can get the fat from your butcher, or save it if you're trimming prime rib before cooking it for your family. Nestle the fat next to the beef shank and cook. The fat melts and soaks into the meat, bringing out all the flavor.

That's the secret of my special laulau. Just between us, OK? No give away the secret now!"

A pressure cooker dramatically reduces the laulau cooking time. If you love laulau and make them often, consider investing in a pressure cooker.

Remove the stiff ribs from the back of the ti leaves. There's no need to steam the leaves, as you are cooking the laulau in a steamer. Do save a couple of the stems; you'll need them to tie up the laulau.

To prepare the lū'au leaves, remove any thick, fibrous ribs or veins. Cut off the stem. You can chop up the stem and put it inside the laulau, or you can save it for stew.

(recipe continued on page 132)

Yield: 1 laulau

½ cups sweet potatoes
   OR 'ulu (breadfruit)
   OR cooked taro
1 pound beef shank (bone
   in, whole)
¼ cup beef fat
6 ti leaves (you'll only use
   4 leaves, but buy extra in
   case you have problems
   removing the ribs)
4 to 5 large lū'au (kalo)
   leaves
Hawaiian salt

Timmy in his taro patch.

TO ASSEMBLE THE LAULAU

Lay down 2 leaves, parallel to each other. Lay 2 leaves across the first 2, forming a large, fat cross. Arrange the lūʻau leaves in a wheel, tips pointing outward.

Put the beef fat in the middle of the lūʻau leaves. Sprinkle the fat with a little Hawaiian salt. Put the beef shank on top of the fat and sprinkle with salt again. Put the sweet potato, ʻulu, or kalo on top of the beef shank.

Wrap the lūʻau leaves around the ingredients, as if you were making a burrito. Pull up the ends of the ti leaves, forming a bag. Tie the bag with 1 or 2 ti leaf stems.

If you have a tiered steamer, put the laulau in a pan to catch the drippings, place in the top tier, and steam for 4 to 5 hours. Keep an eye on the water; don't let the steamer boil dry.

If you have a pressure cooker, put the pan on a stand inside the cooker, add water, seal, and cook for approximately 1 hour.

When the laulau is done, pour the drippings into a container or a fat skimmer. Let the fat rise to the top and skim it off. Save it, don't throw it out.

Unwrap the laulau and discard the ti leaves. Taste a bit of the laulau. Does it need more seasoning? Add salt and some of the skimmed fat if necessary.

Sautéed ʻŌpakapaka with Hāmākua Aliʻi Mushrooms

Chef Perry Bateman, Mama's Fish House, Pāʻia

Yield: 2 servings

"I created this dish to show off our fresh local ʻōpakapaka (pink snapper) and the tasty Big Island mushrooms from Bob and Janice at Hāmākua Mushroom Farms. Once the chopping is done, this dish comes together quickly.

If ʻōpakapaka isn't available, use any firm-fleshed white fish. If you can't find the local mushrooms, substitute button or crimini mushrooms."

Cut up the onion, mushroom, garlic, ginger, and chili pepper per the ingredients list. Cut up the green onion and lemon wedges for the garnish.

Put some white flour in a shallow pan. Season both sides of the ʻōpakapaka with salt and black pepper. Dredge the fish in the pan of flour.

Heat a slick of olive oil in a frying pan over medium heat. When the oil is hot, add the fish. Cook for 1 minute. Add the chopped onion and mushrooms around the fish. Continue cooking the fish.

When one side of the fish has browned, lift the fish from the pan with a spatula. Use a spoon or spatula to scrape the onions and mushrooms into the center of the pan. Put the fish on top of the onions and mushrooms, browned side up. Continue cooking. Lower the heat, if necessary, so that the onions caramelize rather than crisp. The fish, cooking on top, will stay moist.

When the vegetables have begun to caramelize and the fish is almost done, add the garlic, ginger, chili pepper, butter, soy sauce, and white wine and cook to reduce to a tasty sauce.

PRESENTATION

Put the cooked fish on a serving plate and top with the caramelized onions and mushrooms. Sprinkle with the green onion garnish and squeeze a lemon wedge or two over the top. Serve immediately.

¼ cup julienned Maui onion
¾ cup sliced Hāmākua Aliʻi mushroom (¼-inch slices) OR fresh button or crimini mushrooms
2 teaspoons chopped garlic
½ teaspoon minced ginger
1/16 teaspoon seeded and minced Hawaiian chili pepper
2 (6-ounce) ʻōpakapaka fillets (skinless and boneless)
Kosher salt and black pepper
All-purpose white flour for dredging
Olive oil for sautéing
2 tablespoons salted butter
2 teaspoons soy sauce
½ cup white wine

For the garnish:
Sliced green onion
Fresh lemon wedges

Herb Goat Cheese-Stuffed Chicken Breasts

Yield: 4 servings

6 (6-ounce) boneless
  chicken breast halves
6 ounces goat cheese
2 tablespoons unsalted
  butter, softened
1 teaspoons minced chives
1 teaspoon minced parsley
  leaves
1 teaspoon minced fresh
  thyme leaves
¼ teaspoon minced garlic
¼ teaspoon fresh lemon
  juice
Salt
Freshly ground black
  pepper
¼ cup clarified butter or
  vegetable oil

Chef Bev Gannon, Hāli'imaile General Store, Makawao; and Joe's, Wailea

This recipe calls for clarified butter. That's butter that has been cooked over low heat until the milk solids brown and fall to the bottom of the pan. They are filtered out and only the clarified butter is left. It has a higher smoke point than butter, and can be used in frying. If stored in an airtight jar, it will keep without refrigeration for up to a month.

Preheat the oven to 350 degrees.

In a medium-sized mixing bowl, add softened goat cheese, butter, minced herbs and garlic, and lemon juice. Blend together well. Season to taste with salt and pepper.

Divide the goat cheese mixture into 6 equal pieces. Roll the mounds of cheese into 6 cylindrical plugs that will fit inside the pockets in the chicken breasts. Chill 10 minutes to help hold the shape.

Place each chicken breast flat on cutting board. Press firmly down on breast with the palm of one hand. Using a small sharp knife, cut into the breast about ⅓ of the way down the thick side of the breast. Cut into the meat without going through to the other side. Continue cutting until you've cut ¾ of the way down the breast. This cut should form a pocket about 2½ inches long and 1½ to 2 inches deep.

Repeat with the remaining breasts.

Insert 1 cheese plug into each breast. Press to evenly distribute cheese inside pocket. Press edges of breast together to seal. (Use a skewer to sew shut if you want). Lightly season the breasts with salt and freshly ground black pepper.

In a large, oven-proof skillet over medium-high heat, add clarified butter or vegetable oil. When hot, add the chicken breasts skin-side down and sear until golden brown, about 3 minutes. Reduce heat to medium and turn breast over and cook another 3 minutes.

Place the skillet, uncovered, in the preheated oven and bake until the chicken is cooked through, 7 to 10 minutes.

PRESENTATION

Chef Gannon likes to serve these chicken breasts with corn risotto (see the next recipe). Put a generous scoop of risotto in the center of 4 individual serving plates and arrange the chicken along the side. Serve immediately.

Corn Risotto

Chef Bev Gannon, Hāli'imaile General Store, Makawao; and Joe's, Wailea

Yield: 6 servings

"I like to serve this risotto with the chicken breasts from the previous recipe. It's delicious enough that it can stand on its own as well. Try it with grilled fish.

It requires 30 minutes or more of constant stirring. That's standard for risottos. Cook it on a day when you have the time and energy to make a special dish, and you'll see why generations of cooks have decided that risotto is worth the bother."

In a 2-quart saucepan, over medium heat, heat the chicken stock until boiling. Reduce heat to low simmer. Add creamed corn. Leave simmering on back burner.

In a 3-quart saucepan, over medium heat, heat the oil and butter. When the butter has melted, add the shallots and cook, stirring constantly, about 1 minute. Add garlic and stir another 30 seconds.

Raise heat to medium high and add the uncooked rice and cook, stirring constantly, until the grains are opaque, or about 2 to 3 minutes. Add the wine and cook, stirring, until nearly all of the wine has evaporated. Reduce heat to medium.

Begin adding the chicken stock-corn mixture in half-cup increments. After adding stock, stir constantly until nearly all of the stock has evaporated. Add another ½ cup of the stock and cook, stirring, until nearly evaporated. Continue adding stock in this fashion until all the stock has been added, the rice is al dente and the risotto is creamy. Add cream and fresh corn kernels. Keep stirring until mixture is creamy and rice is cooked through. Add ¼ cup of the Parmesan cheese. Blend well. Add salt, pepper, chopped parsley. This whole process may take 18 to 20 minutes.

Remove the risotto from the heat and taste. Adjust the seasoning as necessary. Serve immediately, topping each portion with a sprinkling of the remaining cheese.

Ingredients

- 1 tablespoon olive oil
- 2 tablespoons unsalted butter
- 2 tablespoons finely chopped shallots
- 1 teaspoon minced garlic
- 2 cups Arborio rice
- ¼ cup dry white wine
- 5 cups chicken stock, canned low-sodium chicken broth
- 1 can (about 15 ounces) creamed corn
- ½ cup fresh shucked corn kernels
- ½ cup heavy cream
- ½ cup finely grated Parmesan cheese
- ½ teaspoon salt
- ½ teaspoon freshly ground white pepper
- 1 tablespoon chopped fresh parsley leaves

Onaga Roasted in Ti Leaves

Yield: 4 servings

2 cups diced cooked orange sweet potato (½-inch dice)

1 cup julienned Maui onion

1 cup seeded and diced fresh tomato (¾-inch dice)

8 button or crimini mushrooms, cut into halves or quarters

4 tablespoons sliced green onion

8 basil leaves

4 slices of lemon (¼-inch thick)

4 ti leaves (buy extra leaves; removing the stalk doesn't always go as planned)

4 (6-ounce) onaga fillets (skinless and boneless)

Kosher salt and freshly ground pepper

½ cup salted butter

For the sauce:

4 teaspoons minced garlic

2 teaspoons peeled and minced ginger

¹⁄₁₆ teaspoon minced Hawaiian chili pepper

1 cup white wine

4 teaspoons soy sauce (Yamasa brand)

4 teaspoons Hawaiian chili pepper water

Chef Perry Bateman, Mama's Fish House, Pā'ia

"*T*his dish is inspired by our long Island tradition of baking fresh fish in ti leaves. In the old days, this was done in an imu; for this recipe I bake the fish in a modern oven and spike it with contemporary flavors such as mushrooms and white wine.

This dish is great made with onaga, but you can use any firm-fleshed white fish, such as 'ōpakapaka, monchong, or mahimahi. Go with the freshest and best!"

You probably won't find ti leaves in the supermarket. You may have a plant in your yard, or a friend with a plant. If not, you can substitute banana leaves. You can find them, frozen, in many Asian groceries.

To prepare the sweet potato, boil it, unpeeled, until tender; this should take about 30 minutes. Drain and cool the potato. Peel it, cut it into ½-inch slices and then into ½-inch dice.

Cut up the onion, tomato, mushrooms, green onion, basil, and lemon per the instructions in the ingredients list.

Mince the garlic and ginger for the sauce. Mix all sauce ingredients in a small bowl.

Preheat the oven to 425 degrees.

While it is heating, steam the ti leaves. This is a crucial step. If you omit it, the leaves will burn in the oven. You can use a tiered steamer or just a bowl set on a stand inside a pot partially filled with water.

While the water is coming to a boil, remove the stiff center stalk from the ti leaves. Bend a leaf, slowly, until the stalk pops off the leaf. Peel the rest of it off the leaf, leaving the leaf surface intact. Once you've learned the trick, you will be able to do it ... most of the time. Buy extra leaves, as even the experts have occasional failures. Cut off any remaining stem at the bottom.

Steam the trimmed leaves until they are soft and limp. Remove the leaves and assemble the packets of ti leaf-wrapped fish.

If you don't have any ramekins, you can cook the wrapped fish packets in a large flat baking pan. Wrap the packets inside the pan, pushing them to one side or another to make the space you need to work.

Bake the fish in the 425-degree oven for 10 minutes. Check the fish for doneness; it should be firm and opaque. If the fish isn't fully cooked, and the ti leaf is starting to burn, cover the ramekins or baking pan with a tent of aluminum foil and cook a few minutes longer.

PRESENTATION

Carefully use a wide spatula to remove the ti leaf packages from the baking dish or dishes and slide them into shallow serving bowls. Remove the toothpicks or wooden skewers and open up the ti leaf packets. Remove the ti leaves (they're not edible). Scoop the pan juices out of the baking pans and drizzle over the fish. Serve hot and enjoy!

Tiger-Eye Sushi

Courtesy of Nick's Fishmarket, Maui

W hen George Gomes, now the executive chef at the Mauna Kea Beach Hotel, was the corporate chef at Nick's Fishmarket, Maui, he developed this recipe for the Hawai'i Seafood Challenge. It was a winner and is a staple on the menu. George is tickled that you now have this winning recipe.

To make the beurre blanc sauce, reduce the wine over medium heat until it's almost dry. Watch to make sure it doesn't burn. Whisk in the cream and reduce by half. This will only take a minute. Incorporate the cold butter, one chunk at a time. Add lemon juice and salt and pepper. Whisk all ingredients together and adjust seasoning. Add hot mustard.

To make the relish, cut up the cherry tomatoes and mince the onion.

To make the garnish, trim the kaiware sprouts.

Cook the rice.

To make the tempura batter, whisk all ingredients together until it forms a batter. If it's too thick, add more cold water.

Remove the woody ends from the asparagus. Bring a pot of water to a boil and blanch the asparagus, cooking it only until it turns bright green. Remove it immediately to an ice-water bath, to stop the cooking.

Slit the 'ahi in the middle to make a pocket. Spread wasabi on the bottom of the pocket, add tobiko and asparagus, and top it off with the sushi rice, forming it onto the pocket of ahi. Wrap with the sheet of nori and seal with a dab of water.

Dip the 'ahi roll in tempura batter and fry for 20 seconds. Cut into ½-inch slices and serve with sauce, relish, and garnish.

For the garnish:
¾ ounce kaiware (radish) sprouts (root ends cut off)
¾ ounce pickled ginger

Yield: 6 servings

18 ounces sashimi-grade 'ahi, cut into (6) 3-inch long by 1-inch blocks
6 ounces cooked rice, rolled
6 asparagus spears, blanched
1½ ounces tobiko (flying fish roe)
1 ounce wasabi paste
3 sheets nori
Tempura batter
Salt and pepper to taste

For the beurre blanc sauce:
1 cup white wine
2 tablespoons heavy cream
½ pound unsalted butter, chilled and cut into chunks
1 tablespoon freshly squeezed lemon juice or to taste
Salt & pepper to taste
3 ounces hot mustard

For the tempura batter:
1 cup tempura flour
½ cup soda water
Salt and pepper
½ cup ice cubes

For the relish:
1½ ounce cherry tomatoes, cut in half
1½ ounce minced Kula onion

Mango Gazpacho

Yield: 8 servings

Chef Mark Ellman, Mala Ocean Tavern, Lahaina

4 fresh, very ripe tomatoes (core removed)

1 cup fresh mango pulp

½ green bell pepper, chopped and seeded

¼ Maui onion, peeled and chopped

1 Japanese or hothouse cucumber, peeled and seeded

1 garlic clove, peeled

1 tablespoon peeled, chopped fresh ginger

1 teaspoon toasted fennel seed

¼ bunch fresh mint OR 2 tablespoons dried mint

¼ cup chopped bread, soaked in water and squeezed dry

1 cup canned San Marzano tomatoes

1 cup tomato juice

¼ cup extra virgin olive oil

⅛ cup red wine vinegar

½ teaspoon ground cinnamon

1 teaspoon ground cumin

½ teaspoon ground coriander seeds

1 teaspoon paprika

Salt and pepper to taste

Garnish for each bowl of gazpacho:

1 teaspoon peeled, seeded, and diced cucumber (¼-inch dice)

1 teaspoon diced fresh mango (¼-inch dice)

1 teaspoon seeded and diced fresh tomato (¼-inch dice)

1 teaspoon diced Maui onion (¼-inch dice)

1 teaspoon seeded and diced green pepper (¼-inch dice)

1 teaspoon chopped parsley

½ teaspoon chopped toasted almonds OR macadamia nuts

¼ teaspoon extra virgin olive oil, drizzled on the soup

"*Buy the best produce you can find, or afford, to make the gazpacho. If you don't have access to good fresh tomatoes, I recommend San Marzano canned tomatoes; they're a premium variety, in great demand for authentic Neapolitan pizzas.*"

Prepare the tomatoes, mango, bell pepper, onion, cucumber, garlic, and ginger per the instructions in the ingredients list. Toast the fennel seed in a small pan over medium-high heat. Strip the mint leaves from their stems. Cut up some bread and soak it in water for 1 minute. Pour off any standing water and squeeze out the rest of the water with your hands. You should end up with a thick bread paste.

Mix all ingredients and purée them in a blender or food processor. 2 to 3 minutes should be enough. Pass the soup through a fine sieve, removing any small chunks of vegetable. Store the gazpacho in a covered container and let it chill in the refrigerator overnight. This allows the flavors to develop and mingle.

Chop your garnishes the next day, just before serving, so that they will still be fresh and crisp. The contrast between the silky purée and the crunchy garnish lends character to the dish.

PRESENTATION

Ladle the gazpacho into bowls. Sprinkle each bowl with the prepared garnishes.

Hawaiian BBQ Beef Brisket

Chef Tom Muromoto, Kāʻanapali Beach Hotel, Kāʻanapali

"I remember when, after a long day of spear fishing, the gang would hang out in the backyard, play music, drink beer, cook, and eat all night long. Slack-key players would jam—they were some of the best. We would always look forward to the weekends. Those were the days.

You'll find most if not all of the ingredients for the marinade in your local supermarket (lucky you live Hawaiʻi). You can also shop at Asian groceries.

You can make your own cracked (not ground) pepper by putting peppercorns on the counter and rocking a heavy pan over them.

You'll probably want to start the meat marinating the day before you plan to bake it. Because the meat is baked, then sliced and char-broiled, you can also do the baking the day before you plan to barbeque. Slice the meat, cover, and refrigerate. If you plan ahead, you can minimize fuss on barbeque day."

Cut up the green onions, cilantro, kiwi fruit, garlic, and ginger per the instructions in the ingredients list. Mix all the ingredients for the marinade in a large bowl.

Measure out 2 cups of the marinade and put it in a gallon-size, high-quality, zip-lock plastic bag. Add the brisket and close up the bag. Refrigerate the bag for 4 to 12 hours, turning occasionally so that the brisket is evenly marinated. 4 hours is the minimum; a longer marinating time is better. The rest of the marinade should be put in a covered container or jar and refrigerated as well.

When the brisket is well-marinated and you are ready to cook the brisket, preheat the oven to 325 degrees. Put the meat on a rack in a baking or roasting pan; pour 1 cup of the marinade from the bag into the bottom of the pan. Cover the brisket with aluminum foil; crimp around the edges of the pan. This is called "braising." Bake for approximately 2 hours. Lift the foil and check the internal temperature of the meat. It should be 165 degrees, measured with a meat thermometer. If the meat isn't quite cooked, crimp the foil again and bake a little longer.

When the brisket is done, remove it from the oven and let it rest at room temperature for 30 minutes. Cut the brisket into thin, ¼-inch slices.

Coat the slices with the reserved marinade, the fresh mixture that you set aside in the refrigerator. Heat up the grill and when it's nicely hot, grill the brisket slices. Because they are already cooked, they don't need much time on the grill. Just 2 to 3 minutes on each side. Serve immediately.

Yield: 6 or more servings

5 pounds beef brisket

For the marinade and BBQ basting sauce (Makes 4 cups; use 2 for the marinade, 2 for basting):

- ½ cup chopped green onions
- ½ cup chopped fresh cilantro
- 3 tablespoons peeled and finely chopped kiwi fruit
- 2 tablespoons finely chopped fresh garlic
- 1 tablespoon peeled and grated fresh ginger
- 1 cup soy sauce
- 1 cup granulated sugar
- 1 cup honey
- ½ cup hoisin sauce
- ½ cup gochujang (Korean chili paste)
- ¼ cup Chinese rice wine OR sherry
- ¼ cup plum sauce
- ¼ cup rice wine vinegar
- 2 tablespoons sesame oil
- 1 tablespoon cracked black pepper

Pineapple Grill's Kalbi Short Ribs

Yield: 4 servings

4 pounds of short ribs
    OR 4 (2½ inch cut) kosher
    short ribs, bone-in
3 medium-sized stalks
    celery, chopped
1 medium-sized onion,
    peeled and chopped
1 medium-sized carrot,
    peeled and chopped
2 ounces fresh ginger,
    roughly chopped
4 stalks lemongrass,
    chopped
6 cloves garlic, crushed
Salt and pepper to taste
Kosher salt and freshly
    ground pepper
2 tablespoons olive oil;
    more if needed
8 kaffir lime leaves
1 teaspoon coriander seeds
1 teaspoon whole black
    pepper
9 whole star anise
3 quarts beef or veal stock
    OR beef bouillon

*(ingredients continued on the
next page)*

Chef Ryan Luckey, Pineapple Grill, Kapalua

"Kalbi Short Ribs has been a local favorite for decades. We took a different spin on the classic Azeka's Ribs, using our own style of the Korean kalbi sauce. We perfected the slow cooking of our short rib, using lemongrass, kaffir lime leaf, fresh ginger, garlic, and star anise to bring a distinct flavor. The rich Kalbi demi-glace is a sauce that needs balance, the perfect levels of sweet and savory are key.

I prepared this dish at the Maui Culinary Academy's fundraiser when I was a guest chef. You can use boneless short ribs if you like. I recommend the bone-in ribs, which have more taste. Serve these ribs with Maui Gold Pineapple Salsa (recipe follows)."

Roughly chop the celery, onion, carrot, ginger, lemongrass, and garlic per the ingredient list. These vegetables are going to flavor the broth in which the ribs are cooked; you are not going to serve them.

Season ribs with a nice dusting of kosher salt and black pepper. Add 1 tablespoon of the olive oil to a large pot over medium-high heat. When the oil is hot, add the ribs. Sear each side for about 30 to 45 seconds, or until the ribs are golden-brown. You may need to do this in several batches; don't crowd the pot, or the meat will stew rather than brown. Add more oil if needed to keep the ribs from sticking. Remove the cooked meat and set it to one side.

Keep the heat under the pot at medium-high; add another tablespoon of olive oil. Put the chopped vegetables and the lime leaves, coriander, black pepper, and star anise in the pot and sauté for about 1 to 2 minutes, or until the vegetables have wilted. Add more oil if needed to keep the food from sticking. Put the ribs back into the pot and add the beef stock or bouillon. If the liquid doesn't cover the beef, add water until the meat is covered.

Bring the ribs and broth to a simmer; turn the heat to low and cook for another 2 hours. The meat should be tender and falling off the bone. If it isn't, cook a little longer.

When the ribs are cooked, take out of the stock. If you don't want to bother with the stock, you can discard it. However, you will probably want to filter the stock through a sieve, removing all the vegetable and spice remnants and leaving a highly-seasoned beef broth.

Remove the cooked meat from the bones and discard the bones. You may want to trim off any remaining rib cartilage at this time. Set the meat aside to rest and cool for 10 minutes.

While the meat is resting, make your kalbi sauce. Prepare the chopped green onion and minced ginger per the instructions in the ingredients list. Put the water or stock, sugar, soy sauce, sesame oil, and minced ginger in a small saucepan and bring to a simmer. In another bowl, mix the cornstarch and cold water to make smooth paste. Stir this slurry into the sauce. The sauce will thicken almost instantly. Take the sauce off the heat and add the chopped green onions and the sesame seeds. Check the consistency of the sauce and if it is too thick, add a little water.

Pour the kalbi sauce into a large pan and add the meat from the ribs. Bring the mixture to a simmer; reduce the heat slightly and cook over low heat for about 5 minutes. The meat should be coated with the thick, spicy sauce.

For the kalbi sauce:
½ cup chopped green onion
1 tablespoon peeled and minced fresh ginger
2 cups water
OR stock left over after the ribs have been cooked
2 cups granulated sugar (less if you prefer a stronger soy sauce flavor)
2 cups Aloha low-salt soy sauce
1 tablespoon sesame oil
1 tablespoon toasted white sesame seeds

For the constarch slurry:
2 tablespoons cornstarch
3 tablespoons cold water

Maui Gold Pineapple Salsa

Chef Ryan Luckey, Pineapple Grill, Kapalua

"*I like to heat up this sauce with the chilies in Sriracha sauce or sambal paste. But … not everyone likes it hot, so feel free to leave out the fiery ingredients.*"

Combine all ingredients. Taste and correct the seasoning.

Yield: 6 cups

1 whole pineapple, peeled, cored, and cut into ¼-inch dice
½ cup diced red bell pepper (¼-inch dice)
¼ cup diced red onion (¼-inch dice)
1 tablespoon chopped cilantro
2 or 3 tablespoons lime juice (about 1 average lime)
Sriracha sauce OR sambal paste, to taste (optional)
Sea salt to taste

Seared Opah with Aka Miso Beurre Blanc

Tommy Bahama Tropical Café, Wailea

Yield: 4 servings

A special touch to the seared opah is added with the wonderful beurre blanc sauce, flavored with mirin and miso. Plate the fish with a colorful garnish of black and white sesame seeds and pea shoots.

Pea shoots are the tender leaves of young pea plants, harvested when the plant is just 2 to 4 weeks old. They are fresh, crisp, and bursting with bright "pea" flavor. If you can't find these at the market, you can use any micro-greens (baby greens) or just your favorite lettuce, cut into fine shreds.

You'll want to make the sauce first. Start by preparing the ginger, shallots, and lime juice according to the instructions in the ingredients list.

Measure the white wine and mirin into a small saucepan and add ginger and shallots. Bring the mixture to a boil over medium heat. Reduce the heat slightly, to a simmer, and cook, stirring occasionally, until the liquid has been reduced by half. Add the cream and continue cooking until the liquid is reduced by half again.

Take the stick of butter out of the refrigerator and cut it into small cubes. Add a few cubes of butter to the sauce and whisk to mix. When the butter is soft but not entirely melted, add more butter. Keep adding butter and whisking until all of the butter has been incorporated. If the sauce starts to get too hot, pull the pan off the heat for a minute or two.

When all the butter has been added, remove the saucepan from the heat *immediately*. If you let the sauce continue cooking, the sauce will separate. That is, all the butterfat will melt and float to the top of the sauce.

Add the aka miso and mix with the whisk. Add the lime juice and mix again. Season to taste with salt and pepper.

(recipe continued on page 146)

4 (8-ounce) opah fillets
Salt and pepper to taste
4 tablespoons olive oil

For the aka miso beurre blanc:
2 tablespoons fresh ginger, thinly sliced and smashed with the flat side of a clever
1 tablespoon peeled and minced shallots
1 tablespoon fresh lime juice
½ cup dry white wine
½ cup mirin
1 cup heavy whipping cream (36% butterfat)
½ cup (1 stick) chilled unsalted butter, cut into small cubes
1½ tablespoons aka miso paste (red miso paste)
salt and white pepper to taste

For the garnish:
8 sprigs of pea shoot
½ tablespoon mixed black and white sesame seeds
summer vegetables (or favorite vegetables)

Pour the sauce through a fine strainer or sieve to remove any lumps or chunks of shallot and ginger. Cover the sauce to keep it warm while you cook the fish. If possible, avoid having to reheat the sauce on the stove, as it will be difficult to do so without overheating the sauce and causing it to separate.

To cook the fish, season both sides of the opah fillets with salt and pepper to your taste. Heat the olive oil in a large sauté pan over medium-high heat. When the oil is very hot (but not smoking) add the fish fillets. Sear the fillets until they are golden brown on one side; flip the fillets and sear the other side. Do not overcook the fish; you want the middle of the fillets to be not quite fully cooked at the end of this first step. This will take approximately 2 minutes on each side.

Remove the pan from the heat. The residual heat in the pan will finish cooking the opah. The fish will be fully cooked but not dry.

PRESENTATION

Serve this opah with freshly cooked rice or couscous, and a side salad. 'Ono in its own way!

Moi Poke, Lomilomi-Style

Chef Perry Bateman, Mama's Fish House, Pā'ia

Yield: 2 servings

"*Moi is one of my favorite fishes. There's a reason that it was reserved for Hawaiian royalty—it has such rich flavor. That's why I like to make poke with moi. I do it in the old style, very traditional, without soy sauce and sesame oil. They're good, but not for this fish. All it needs is līpoa seaweed, 'inamona, chili pepper, and Hawaiian salt. Remember: after the poke is mixed, lomilomi it to release the fats and flavor in the moi. It gets slightly mushy, but the flavor is sublime.*"

You can often buy 'inamona at the fish counter. If you can't find it, mashed roasted salted cashews can be substituted.

Cut up the moi, onion, and green onion. Rinse the līpoa until it is completely free of sand and coral bits. Chop the seaweed and chili pepper. If substituting cashews for the 'inamona, crush the cashews with a mortar and pestle.

Put the moi, salt, onion, green onion, and līpoa in a medium bowl and mix with a serving spoon or very very clean hands. Use your hands or the spoon to mash the fish a little, releasing oils and flavor. Taste. You may want to add more salt but … be careful. You're going to sprinkle the poke with the 'inamona, which also contains salt.

Put the poke in a serving bowl and sprinkle with 'inamona.

- 1 pound fresh moi, cut into ¼- or ½-inch dice (remove skin or leave it on, as you like)
- 2 teaspoons Hawaiian salt or to taste
- 4 tablespoons diced Maui onion (¼-inch dice)
- 2 tablespoons sliced green onion (¼-inch pieces)
- 1 tablespoon finely chopped līpoa seaweed
- ¼ teaspoon seeded and minced Hawaiian chili pepper, or to taste (optional, but recommended)
- ½ teaspoon 'inamona (roasted kukui nut mashed with salt)

Potato-Scaled Mahimahi

Yield: 4 servings

4 (6-ounce) mahimahi fillets
1 large Yukon Gold potato
4 tablespoons olive oil, for
  sautéing

For the beurre rouge sauce:
4 cups red wine, reduced to
  consistency of syrup
2 tablespoons honey
8 ounces butter, chilled and
  cut into pieces
1 lemon, juiced; you will
  probably not use all the
  juice
Salt and pepper to taste

*For the truffle mashed
  potatoes:*
4 large Yukon Gold
  potatoes, boiled and
  mashed
2 tablespoons extra-virgin
  olive oil
2 ounces butter
1 tablespoon white truffle
  oil
Salt to taste

For the garnish:
20 stalks asparagus,
  blanched (see directions
  on page 139)
4 basil leaves

Chef Geno Sarmiento, Nick's Fishmarket, Wailea

*T*he famous French chef Paul Bocuse popularized the use of potato "scales" to top a fish fillet. Not only were the scales a witty visual reference to fish scales, they cooked up in a delicious way, adding a tasty crunch to the moist fish inside.

I like to serve these 'onolicious fillets with a beurre rouge sauce, accompanied by blanched asparagus spears and truffled mashed potatoes. If you're short on time and energy, you can prepare the fish scales and the wine reduction ahead of time, sauté the fish and prepare the sauce at the last minute, and serve with rice and a simple salad.

Note that beurre rouge sauces can be tricky. If you're not used to making them, it is easy to over-heat them, so that the sauce "breaks." That is, the butter melts and separates out into an oily layer on top. You can rescue a broken sauce by chilling it while you cook a pint or so of heavy cream until it has reduced by ¾. Slowly whisk the chilled and broken sauce into the cream. You must also do this if you want to re-use leftover beurre rouge sauce. You cannot reheat the sauce without breaking it, so you will have to fold the chilled sauce into reduced cream, turning it into a sauce Nantais.

Put the 4 cups of red wine into a saucepan and bring to a simmer, stirring occasionally, until most of the water and alcohol have evaporated and the wine has become a thick syrup. Turn off the heat when the reduction is finished.

While the wine is reducing, prepare the fish. Peel the potato and cut it into thin, even slices, about 1/16-inch thick. Start from the narrow end of the potato, so that you are cutting long ovals rather than rounds. In restaurant kitchens, we use a mandolind, a hand-operated slicer and grater.

Season fish with salt and pepper. Place the basil leaves on top of the fish, then overlap the potato slices to resemble scales.

Peel, boil, and rice the Yukon Gold potatoes. Add the butter and truffle oil. Mash by your favorite method and salt to taste. Put the mashed potatoes in a covered, oven-safe dish and hold them in an oven on low heat.

(recipe continued on page 150)

Before cooking the fish, finish the beurre rouge sauce by heating the red wine reduction over medium heat and stirring in the honey. When the honey has dissolved, add chunks of chilled butter (slowly at first, faster as the sauce heats and thickens), whisking as you add. You must keep the heat low and whisk constantly. If the butter melts, it will separate from the sauce. You want to soften the butter, not melt it. When all the butter has been added, remove the sauce from the heat and season to taste with fresh lemon juice, pepper, and salt. If for some reason you must keep the sauce warm for more than a few minutes, you can do so in a double boiler over hot but not boiling water.

If the sauce breaks, you can repair it with a pint of cream; see the directions in the head note.

To prepare the fish, heat the olive oil in a large sauté pan over medium-high heat. When the olive is hot, turn down the heat to medium and add the fillets, potato-side down. The starch from the potatoes will adhere to the fish. Cook until the potatoes are lightly browned, about 3 minutes. Turn the fish over and finish cooking. Do be careful not to overcook the fish, which will then be tough and dry.

Once the fish has started sautéing, blanch the asparagus according to the directions on page 139.

PRESENTATION

You can serve your meal restaurant-style, on 4 individual plates. I like to put mashed potatoes in the middle of the plate and arrange the asparagus spears over the potatoes. I pour the beurre rouge sauce around the potatoes. A potato-scaled mahi-mahi fillet tops the asparagus, scale-side up.

However, this fish is also delicious served family-style, on a platter with a drizzling of beurre rouge over the top.

Banana Caramel Eruption

Chef Tom Muromoto, Kāʻanapali Beach Hotel, Kāʻanapali

Yield: 2 servings

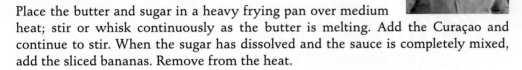

*T*his dish won Best in Show at the 2002 Taste of Lahaina festival. A delicious Curaçao-flavored banana-caramel sauce lifts brownies and ice cream (already great) to new heights.

You can use bakery brownies for this dessert or you can bake your own brownies, using your favorite recipe.

Place the butter and sugar in a heavy frying pan over medium heat; stir or whisk continuously as the butter is melting. Add the Curaçao and continue to stir. When the sugar has dissolved and the sauce is completely mixed, add the sliced bananas. Remove from the heat.

Microwave the brownies for 30 seconds or less. They should be warm but not hot.

Set out 2 serving plates. Put 1 brownie in the center of each plate; top each brownie with 1 cup of macadamia nut ice cream. Pour half the banana-caramel sauce over each brownie. Top each treat with whipped cream and a sprinkling of the chopped macadamia nuts.

4 tablespoons unsalted butter, softened
6 tablespoons brown sugar
1 cup sliced bananas
2 teaspoons orange Curaçao liqueur
2 (3 x 3-inch square) chocolate fudge brownies
2 cups macadamia nut ice cream
2 tablespoons chopped roasted macadamia nuts
4 tablespoons whipped cream

'Ahi Poke Hawaiian-Style

Yield: 6 to 8 as an
appetizer

1 pound sashimi-grade 'ahi,
  cut into ¾-inch dice
1 medium-sized tomato,
  trimmed and cut into
  ¼-inch dice
½ cup Maui onion, peeled
  and chopped
2 tablespoons soy sauce
1 teaspoon sesame oil
½ teaspoon granulated
  sugar
½ teaspoon red chili
  pepper flakes
  OR 1 Hawaiian chili
  pepper, trimmed and
  minced
2 tablespoons green onion,
  chopped, for garnish

Chef Sam Choy, Sam Choy's Breakfast, Lunch & Crab, Honolulu

This dish typifies contemporary Hawaiian-style poke. It blends traditional Hawaiian ingredients ('ahi, Hawaiian salt, limu kohu) with Asian touches (soy sauce, sesame oil) to create a multi-cultural blend of flavors. I've always maintained that Hawai'i is at the crossroads of the culinary universe; this simple but tasty dish is case in point. And the sweet Maui onion gives it just the right taste.

Combine the 'ahi, tomato, onion, soy sauce, sesame oil, sugar, and the red chili pepper flakes or minced chili pepper. Mix well. Allow flavors to blend for 1 hour before serving. Garnish with the chopped green onion before serving.

Community Recipes

Maui is known for a populace that enjoys cooking. I am always amazed at the good things coming out of my neighbors' and friends' kitchens. Some of their recipes have become part of my cooking bible. But it's impossible for one person, even a chef, to know everything about Maui cooking. What makes it even more challenging is that some recipes exist in different versions, others are rarely shared, and still others are never written down but passed on by word of mouth. So I asked my good friend, Gail Ainsworth, who has been both a local historian and a local foodie for a very long time, to gather up some of the oldies but goodies. Gail went even further, documenting people's fond memories of former favorite restaurants. Some of these places are big, some are small, but they all serve great food. The result is amazing as you will see and, enjoy.

This chapter takes readers back to some classic ways of thinking about Maui food. Looking back at yesterday's recipes that are still popular today helps us to remember past generations and remind us that on Maui we are one big community.

Maui's microclimates provide a nourishing environment for fruit, vegetables, and livestock, and the surrounding ocean has lent its distinctive taste to Maui limu and fish. Like SPAM and rice, food and Maui just go together. Hearty cabbage, sweet gentle onions, yellow sweet potatoes, and bright persimmons all grow to perfection in Kula farms. The entire island awaits the superb mangos available seasonally in Lahaina. Liliko'i and guava edge the roads of East Maui, free for the picking, and laden breadfruit trees tempt drivers on the road to Hāna. Outstanding recent additions include red-ripe strawberries grown in Kula; prizewinning East Maui goat cheese; Upcountry coffee rivaling Kona's best; and healthy and hearty beef from cattle grazing the vast acreage of six Maui ranches.

Sugar and pineapple still blanket Maui, the only island to retain these traditional crops. And these products have improved and expanded. Hāli'imaile Pineapple Company grows Maui Gold, a surprisingly sweet fruit, and Hawaiian Commercial & Sugar Company has developed a series of specialty sugars.

It is no wonder that Mauians of all ethnicities are good cooks and enthusiastic eaters.

—Gail Ainsworth

Won Tons

Yield: approximately forty
   won tons

½ pound ground pork
6 water chestnuts, minced
½ teaspoon salt
1 teaspoon oyster sauce
¼ teaspoon monosodium
   glutamate
1 stalk green onion, minced
1 package won ton pi
   (wrappers)

Ah Fook's Super Market (Kahului)

Ah Fook's Super Market, founded in 1917 by Tam Ah Fook, continues to serve Maui cooks, stocking ingredients for any Asian cuisine desired. Its large store burned down in 2005, but a smaller store still keeps up its special mission of keeping local products available. Ah Fook's Super Market handed this recipe out to customers decades ago.

Combine all the ingredients, except the won ton pi, in a large bowl and mix well. Hold a won ton pi on the palm of the left hand and place about ⅛ of a teaspoon of the mixture in the center of the wrapper. Fold the won ton pi into a triangle, taking the closest corner and folding it toward the opposite corner. Seal by dampening the corners with a little water and press with the thumb and forefinger. Then bring the other two ends together and seal.

Heat a skillet with enough oil for deep-frying to about 360 degrees. Drop the won ton into the hot oil and fry until light brown, making sure the filling is done. Drain absorbent paper. Serve crispy as a pūpū.

Variation: May be used in sai mein (saimin) to make won ton mein, or in other soups. For soups, drop won ton in boiling water and cook until it floats. Note: If preparing won ton for soups, add a little more filling, about ¼ teaspoon, making the total a little less than ½ teaspoon.

Ah Fook Super Market staff, 1963.

Maui Gold Grilled Fresh Pineapple

Hāli'imaile Pineapple Company & Maui Culinary Academy

*O*nly Maui grows Maui Gold pineapple, which has a rich golden color, is low in acid, and has three times the vitamin C of regular pineapple. It is said to be the sweetest pineapple ever grown and gets sweeter once grilled.

Yield: 12 pūpū-sized
  servings

1 Maui Gold pineapple

Prepare grill. Cut pineapple lengthwise through crown, keeping crown attached. Cut each half in half, repeating until there are eight wedges. Grill pineapple wedges, alternating cut sides down, on a lightly oiled rack set five to six inches over glowing coals until just charred, about two minutes on each side.

To serve, cut fruit from shell with a sharp knife. Leaving fruit wedge resting on the shell, cut each wedge into bite-sized pieces.

Chicken Skin Sitsaron or Chicharon

Maria Gamponia (Wailuku)

*S*onny Gamponia, Maria's son, feels that Colonel Sanders could make a fortune if he served this in his restaurants.

Yield: approximately 25
  pieces

Skin from 1 chicken
1 cup Crisco
2 to 3 tablespoons chicken
  lard

Separate the skin from the chicken and cut into small pieces. Blot any water from the pieces of skin to assure crispness. Salt and deep-fry in a small frying pan using Crisco and 2 to 3 tablespoons rendered chicken fat until golden brown and crispy. Fry only 2 to 3 pieces at a time.

RENDERED CHICKEN FAT

Remove fat from the chicken and put it into a saucepan. Cook on low heat with a little bit of water (¼ cup) until the fat is melted. Put this rendered chicken fat into a jar to be used as needed.

Maria and Demetrio Gamponia wedding, 1946.

Salads

Lazy Namasu

Yield: 4 servings

2 tablespoons Hawaiian salt
¼ cup sugar
¼ cup Japanese vinegar
3 cucumbers, thinly sliced

Mildred Mizoguchi (Kahului)

*T*his recipe and the next were handwritten by Mildred Mizoguchi on the back of pineapple can labels. She served the dishes to her children and grandchildren over the decades.

Soak, squeeze, eat.

Mildred and Jimmy Mizoguchi and family, ca. 1961.

Somen Salad

Yield: 6 servings

1 package somen noodles
Iceberg lettuce, finely
    shredded (optional)
1 carrot, sliced
1 to 2 stalks celery, sliced
1 block kamaboko, sliced
1 to 2 cucumbers, seeded
    and sliced
Char siu, slivered (optional)
1 egg
Ajitsuke nori or furikake
    (optional)

*For the somen dressing
    (combine and pour in
    bottle):*
1 tablespoon olive oil
2 tablespoons sesame oil
¼ cup Japanese vinegar
½ cup white sugar
½ cup soy sauce
Dash of dashi-no-moto
    (optional)

Natsue Kametani (Kula)

*N*atsue Kametani is well-known as an excellent baker and cook and has passed the tradition on to her family. This recipe is one of her favorites.

Boil somen: rinse, drain and put on platter. Sprinkle lettuce over somen. Place carrots, celery, kamaboko, and char siu over somen. Beat egg, fry, slice into strips and place over vegetables. Scatter nori over vegetables and egg. Chill. Pour dressing over somen before serving.

Noted Kula cook and baker Natsue Kametani.

Korean-Style Ogo

Miles Lee & Cynthia Lee Smith (Kula)

Yield: 6 servings

The following three recipes came from Miles' and Cynthia's grandmothers, who emigrated from Korea. The recipes have evolved over the years due to the creativity of family members and the influence of other ethnicities here in Hawai'i.

Cynthia Lee Smith with her mother Dora Woo Lee.

Boil 3 or 4 quarts of water. Submerge the ogo for 5 to 6 seconds and drain in a colander. Rinse under cold water to stop the cooking process. Shake out excess water but don't over do it. A small amount of water should remain. Add all ingredients together and mix well.

If preferred, add chopped tomatoes and/or a finely sliced sweet Maui onion to the mix.

1 bag ogo (Moloka'i ogo works well as it has a fine texture)
1 large jalapeno pepper, sliced thin
¼ cup soy sauce
¼ cup mirin
¼ cup rice vinegar or, if available, Korean apple vinegar (Korean apple vinegar is available at Seoul Market on Lower Main Street)
1 tablespoon chopped green onion
tomatoes, chopped (optional)
Maui onion, finely sliced (optional)

Japanese Pickled Cabbage

Mildred Mizoguchi (Kahului)

This recipe can also be used with daikon, mustard cabbage, or cucumber.

Heat the salt, vinegar, sugar, and water until they dissolve. Let solution cool before pouring on cabbage in jar. Turn cabbage over occasionally or overturn jar. Wait 2 days.

Serves 12

Kula head cabbage, cut in quarters, and placed in jar
¼ cup Hawaiian salt
¼ cup cider vinegar
¾ cup raw sugar
4 cups water

Korean Salad Dressing

Yield: about ½ cup

Miles Lee and Cynthia Lee Smith (Kula)

2 tablespoons soy sauce
2 tablespoons Korean apple vinegar or other light vinegar
2 tablespoons water
1 teaspoon powdered chili pepper
1 teaspoon honey or sugar (mirin for less sweetness)
1 teaspoon crushed, roasted sesame seeds

*T*his recipe can be used to perk up any green salad as it has a characteristic Korean spiciness.

Combine all ingredients, mix well, and toss with red leaf lettuce just before serving.

Dora Woo Lee and family.

Tofu with Kim Chee

Yield: 4 servings as a salad

Dora Woo Lee and Cynthia Lee Smith (Kula)

1 (14-ounce) block firm tofu, cut in cubes or sliced
2 tablespoons soy sauce
2 tablespoons sesame oil
1 cup kim chee, chopped (it doesn't matter what kind) Use more or less to taste
1 tablespoon toasted sesame seeds for garnish

*M*rs. Lee's daughter, Cynthia Smith, says that this is an easy and popular way to eat tofu, served as a salad. The Smiths love this and eat it often. They sometimes make a meal of it with hot rice or cold noodles.

Arrange tofu on a platter or in shallow dish. Mix soy sauce and sesame oil and pour over tofu. Spoon kim chee over tofu. Sprinkle sesame seeds over all. Serve cold.

Entrées

Miso Pot Roast Pork

Yoshie Watanabe (Wailuku/Kula)

Yield: 8 servings

Yoshie Watanabe has been named grand champion nine times at the Maui County Fair for her combined scores in cooking, baking, crocheting, and sewing.

Place pork in a large sauce pan. Combine remaining ingredients and pour over pork. Cover and simmer for 2½ to 3 hours, turning frequently to evenly season pork. Add more stock or water as needed. Skim off fat and serve sauce with pork.

5 pounds pork butt
½ cup miso
½ cup soy sauce
2 cups of chicken stock or water
½ cup HC&S Maui Brand raw sugar
1 small piece ginger, crushed
2 cloves garlic, crushed

Roast Turkey Chinese-Style

Ah Fook's Super Market (Kahului)

Yield: 8 servings

Giving out recipes was common at Ah Fook's in the 1950s and 1960s. Fortunately this one was saved by an employee so we can still enjoy it.

T. S. Shinn, Margaret Tam, and Jimmy Mizoguchi of Ah Fook Super Market.

Clean bird and wipe dry. Combine sauce ingredients and rub the outside of the bird with it. Let it stand for 30 minutes, turning several times. Pour the mixture into the cavity of the bird and lace up tight. Brush bird with oil. Wrap bird in aluminum foil and place in roasting pan with breast facing up. Roast in oven at 325 degrees, allowing 20 minutes per pound. About 20 minutes before it is scheduled to be done, open the foil for the remaining time to brown the skin. Serve with the sauce removed from the cavity of the bird, adding oyster sauce and monosodium glutamate.

1 turkey, 10 to 12 pounds

For the sauce:
3 tablespoons wine or whiskey
½ cup soy sauce
2 to 3 stalks green onion, cut to 2-inch lengths
½ cup brown sugar, packed tight
¼ cup bean sauce
1 small piece ginger, crushed
¼ teaspoon heong liu fun (Chinese five spice)
3 cloves garlic, crushed

1 tablespoon oyster sauce
½ teaspoon monosodium glutamate

Kau Yoke (Kau Yuk)

Yield: 6 servings

Mae Ching Santos (Olowalu)

2 pounds belly pork
1 teaspoon ginger juice
2 medium potatoes or
   Chinese taro
1 teaspoon brown sugar
1 teaspoon thick soy sauce
2 tablespoons red bean
   curd
1 teaspoon Chinese five
   spice
1 teaspoon salt
1 clove garlic, crushed
2 teaspoons water

*T*his recipe and the following one were part of an adult education class Mae Ching Santos taught at Lahainaluna in 1957 to some of the leading citizens of Lahaina.

Mae Ching Santos with her sister Rose and brother-in-law David Wong.

Boil belly pork in 2 quarts of water for 35 minutes. Remove pork and let it stand under running water until it is cooled. Wipe dry and rub with thick soy sauce. Fry in hot oil until brown. Remove and soak in cold running water.

Slice pork. Peel potatoes or taro and cut into pieces about 2 inches by 1½ inches by ½-inch. Mix garlic, brown sugar, Chinese five spice, red bean curd, ginger juice, and water. Add sliced pork and mix well.

Place a piece of pork and a slice of potato alternately into a large bowl and steam for 1½ to 2 hours.

Sweet-Sour Pig's Feet

Yield: 4 to 8 servings

1 pair pig's feet (medium-
   sized)
1 cup vinegar
½ cup brown sugar (or
   sugar to taste)
1½ to 2 cups water
2 teaspoons salt
1 teaspoon soyu
3 tablespoons Chinese
   brown bean sauce

Mae Ching Santos (Olowalu)

Cut pig's feet into small chunks. Put oil in pan and add pig's feet. Fry until slightly brown then add vinegar, brown sugar, water, and seasoning. Cook 1½ to 2 hours until tender, stirring occasionally.

George Santos preparing a pig.

Pā'ia Plantation Chicken Soup

Jackie Pias Carlin (Kīhei)   Yield: 8 to 10 servings

*T*his is both a recipe and a picture of a plantation past. Jackie has written of her early years in Pā'ia's Orpheum Camp in her book Spirit of the Village *and has taught Filipino cooking. In Jackie's words:*

"When I think of food from Maui's past, I think of the chicken soup from my Pā'ia childhood.

Soup was made from a retired hen or the unfortunate rooster from the afternoon's chicken fight. The bird was chopped into bite-sized pieces and placed into the pot with fresh water, a huge slice of fresh ginger, and some garlic. After the water came to a light boil, it simmered for at least four hours or until the meat easily fell off the bone.

Jackie Pias Carlin celebrating her fifth birthday with parents Rose and Balbino Pias and family.

While the soup cooked, the adults chose what the additional ingredient would be. The choices at the time were green papaya, marunggay leaves (horseradish tree), or bittermelon leaves. Since all these were growing in our backyard, we used whatever was plentiful that afternoon. Generally only one of these additional ingredients was used, though the taste of papaya and marunggay went together well and could be paired. To use papaya, we chose the greenest and the hardest; peeled, seeded, and cut into pieces. When using either of the leaves, pick triple to quadruple the amount that can be snugly held in one palm. If we picked marunggay leaves, the women sat around the table and plucked the leaves off the stems after snapping them off the tree. Since I loved bittermelon so much, my aunt taught me at a young age how to harvest it by pinching only the most tender leaves and shoots off the ends of the vine.

Flavor the soup with 2 teaspoons of patis (fish sauce), or to taste, before adding the papaya, marunggay, or bittermelon leaves. The chunks of papaya or leaves were gently dropped into the soup just before serving so the papaya was tender but not mushy, and the leaves could quickly melt over the hot soup. The result is a rich broth served in a cup for sipping.

Green papaya, marunggay or bittermelon are available in Filipino markets, and chicken broth is available in cans or cartons, but it's not the same as making one's own from scratch."

Sunday Dinner Chicken Adobo

Yield: 4 to 6 servings

Maria Gamponia (Wailuku)

1 chicken, cut in small
  pieces
1 teaspoon salt
  OR 1 tablespoon soy
  sauce
3 cloves garlic
½ teaspoon black whole
  peppercorns
2 bay leaves
⅛ cup vinegar
1 cup water, chicken broth,
  beer, or coconut milk
Vegetable oil

*F*ilipinos often raised chickens in their backyard, as the Gamponia family did. Sonny Gamponia describes what happened on Sunday in his house. "Sunday was always the day Mom would slaughter a chicken. When I went into the kitchen for breakfast, there would be a big pot of hot water, in which the chicken had been dunked to loosen the feathers. The smell of wet feathers permeated the room and the plucked chicken sat in a bowl with blood draining down the sink." The Sunday chicken was ready to cook.

Place chicken in saucepan with oil. Add salt, garlic, peppercorns, bay leaf, vinegar, and water. Cook at a high heat, then turn the burner down, cover, add a few chunks of pork and pork fat for flavor, and simmer until chicken is tender and liquid is evaporated.

As dishes many evolve over time, Maria Gamponia's son, Demetrio Gamponia Jr., also known as Sonny, has modernized the recipe. He has eliminated the pork and pork fat and cooks with boneless chicken. Here is his revised recipe.

Place chicken in saucepan. Add bay leaf, vinegar, salt, garlic, and peppercorns and vinegar. Cook at high heat until the mixture simmers, then turn the heat down until the liquid reduces and the chicken is poached and tender. Separate the chicken and the liquid. Brown the chicken in a little bit of vegetable oil. Pour the cooking liquid over the chicken and add ½ cup to 1 cup of water to make a thin sauce. Heat through.

Sonny says that having the chicken in sauce tastes better and much like the adobo found in the Philippines. He said he ordered a chicken dish at Gerard's in Lahaina a decade ago, and it tasted just like chicken adobo but, of course, it was French.

Sunday dinner with the Gamponia and Aquilizan families.

Granny's Hawaiian-Style Stew

Helen Leina'ala Watson Shaw (Wailuku)

Yield: 8 servings

*I*n the Hawaiian way, Robbie St. Sure Lum learned this recipe and the next by working with her granny, Helen Shaw, in the kitchen. Robbie was a boarder at Kamehameha Schools and, whenever she would come home to Maui on vacation, her granny would have a big pot of the following stew ready with poi, quartered Maui onion with Hawaiian salt, and chili pepper water. Depending on the time of year, they would also have līpoa cut up and sprinkled over the stew. The meal always ended with cold cut-up mango. Hawaiian comfort food!

In a large pot, sauté onions, garlic, and ½ cup celery with leaves. Remove. Add oil to pan and coat stew meat and brisket with flour and brown well. The more crispy and brown the meat is, the more ono the stew will be. Return sautéed vegetables to pot. Then add Worcestershire sauce, soy sauce, water, chicken broth, tomato sauce, bouillon, and bay leaves. Cook until meat is tender, about an hour. Add carrots, celery and potato and cook until done. Add cornstarch mixture to thicken. Add salt and pepper to taste.

2 pounds brisket meat, bone-in
2 pounds boneless meat
1 Maui onion, cut in wedges
5 cloves garlic, gently smashed
½ cup celery, including the leaf
1 cup flour
2 tablespoons Worcestershire sauce
2 tablespoons soy sauce
2 cups water
1 can chicken broth
1 small can tomato sauce
4 beef bouillon cubes
2 small bay leaves
5 carrots, chunked
2 stalks of celery, in large slices
3 large potatoes, chunked
4 tablespoons cornstarch mixed well with a little cold water

Kalo Beef Stew

Robbie St. Sure Lum (Wailuku)

Yield: 6 servings

Add oil to a large pot. Coat stew meat and brisket with flour, Hawaiian salt, and pepper and sear in hot oil until crispy. Add water with beef bouillon to cover. Simmer until tender, about an hour. Add lū'au leaves (below) and, if desired, kalo.

Prepare lū'au leaves by separating the stalk from the leaves. Remove the thin fibrous skin of the stalk and discard. Cut up the remainder of the stalk and add to the leaves. Put lū'au leaves and stalk in a pot of boiling water with Hawaiian salt added. Boil gently for 5 to 10 minutes until leaves wilt. Throw out cooking water and rinse again. Boil again in water with a pinch of baking soda added. Cook 30 minutes until tender but not mushy. This process will remove the sting in the taste.

Helen Shaw in her Wailuku yard, 1940s.

2 pounds brisket stew meat, bone-in
2 pounds boneless stew meat
1 cup flour
Hawaiian salt
pepper
2 cups water
4 beef bouillon cubes
1 bunch lū'au leaves
Kalo, cut in 2-inch chunks and cooked until tender (optional)

Side Dishes

Portuguese Pickled Bacalhau

Yield: 6 small servings

Morlee Walters (Waikapū)

1 pound salted codfish
(soak from 12 to 14 hours
in cold water, changing
water from 2 to 3 times
to remove some of the
salt)
1 Maui onion, thinly sliced
1 bunch flat leaf (Italian)
parsley, chopped
Hot pepper (optional)

Dressing:
¼ cup olive oil
¼ cup cider vinegar (or to
taste)

*L*ong ago, Granny Ernestine Mendonça passed this recipe on to her granddaughter, Morlee Walters, who has kept the recipe alive by making and sharing it, stating that it is her favorite Portuguese recipe. Morlee warns us that this is not a dish to eat before a first date. Dried codfish is available at local markets.

Steam fish for 15 to 20 minutes. Remove meat from the bones and tear into bite-sized flakes. Put onion, parsley, and fish into a bowl. Heat olive oil and vinegar just to boiling and pour over fish and vegetable mixture. Let cool. Cover and store in refrigerator overnight.

Serve with hot boiled potatoes (Irish or sweet) or bread. It goes especially well as a pūpū with beer.

Mendonça family, with oldest child Ernestine, in 1918.

Boiled Breadfruit

Yield: 4 servings

Bonnie Tuell (Makawao)

4 cups green breadfruit,
diced
6 cups water
1 teaspoon salt
Salt, pepper, and butter (to
taste)

*B*onnie spent many years as a home economist at Maui Electric Company and is the author of popular local cookbooks.

Boil water, add salt and breadfruit and boil until tender—about one hour. Drain and add salt, pepper, and butter.

Home economist Bonnie Tuell in her Maui Electric Company uniform.

Gandule Rice

Louise Galacia Pacheco Martelles (Kahului)

Yield: 14 small servings

*g*andule rice is served every year as part of the popular plate lunch sold by the Maui Puerto Rican Association at the Maui County Fair. The plate also includes bacalao (codfish) salad and pasteles.

Place 1 can (liquid included) gandule beans in a large pot and add 1½ cups water. Bring to a boil. Brown pork in vegetable oil in skillet. Add onion, bell pepper, cilantro, oregano, garlic, cumin, curry, tomato sauce, salt, and pepper. Add 3¼ cups of water and simmer. When mixture comes to a boil, add achiote oil. Stir until well mixed. Wash and drain rice. Add all ingredients, including rice, to the boiling beans and stir well. Cover and simmer for 8 to 10 minutes. Stir mixture again. Cover and turn heat down to low for 15 minutes. Add olives if desired. Serve hot.

2 pounds pork, cubed
1 (15-ounce) can gandule beans (pigeon peas)
4¾ cups water
4 tablespoons vegetable oil
1 medium onion, diced
¾ cup bell pepper, diced
3 heaping tablespoons cilantro, chopped
2 teaspoons oregano
3 heaping tablespoons garlic, chopped
½ teaspoon cumin
½ teaspoon curry powder
1 (8-ounce) can tomato sauce
2 tablespoons salt (or to taste)
1½ teaspoons black pepper (or to taste)
6¼ cups medium-grain white rice
½ cup achiote oil, recipe on page 168 (may substitute annatto powder or sazon achiote powder)
½ (15-ounce) can black olives (optional)

Louise Martelles with her daughter Bobbi Pagan and great-granddaughter B-Love Pagan.

Homemade Achiote Oil

Yield: 1 cup

Louise Galacia Pacheco Martelles (Kahului)

1 cup vegetable oil
½ cup achiote seeds

*A*chiote oil may also be purchased ready-to-use.

Combine oil and achiote seeds in a saucepan. Over medium -ow heat, bring to a boil, stirring occasionally, until oil turns red in color. Turn the heat off and let stand for about an hour. Drain and discard seeds. Cool thoroughly. Refrigerate and use when needed.

Imitation Crab Patties with Tofu

Yield: 6 servings

Natsue Kametani (Kula)

1 (14-ounce) block of firm tofu, well drained
1 (10-ounce) package imitation crab
2 eggs
¼ cup mayonnaise
¼ cup string beans, chopped
¼ cup Kula onions, chopped
3 tablespoons green onions, chopped
¼ cup carrots, grated
Seasoned salt and pepper to taste

*T*his recipe is one that appeals to just about everybody.

Mix all ingredients together. Shape into patties and fry in skillet on medium heat.

Natsue Kametani with children Carol, Joan, Grace, Kay, Ricky, and Avis.

Desserts

Pineapple Pie

Yoshie Watanabe (Wailuku/Kula)

Yield: 6 to 8 servings

*T*his recipe won first place in the Hawai'i State Crisco American Pie Celebration in 1990. Maui Gold pineapple didn't exist in 1990, but using these new low-acid sweet fruit grown by Hāli'imaile Pineapple Company would make the pie even more of a delectable treat.

To make the pie crust, sift dry ingredients, cut in shortening until crumbly. Add milk, make into a ball, and roll out on floured board. Place in a 9-inch pie plate. Flute and prick generously with fork. Bake in hot oven at 450 degrees for 15 minutes or until brown. Cool.

To make the filling, soak gelatin in pineapple juice. Beat 4 egg yolks until light, gradually adding sugar. Stir in pineapple and lemon juice. Cook and stir until thickened. Stir in gelatin until dissolved. Cool until mixture is almost set.

Whip 4 egg whites until stiff, sugar, salt, and cream of tartar. Fold egg-white mixture gently into pineapple mixture. Fill pie shell and chill. Top with whipped cream. Garnish and serve.

For the pie crust:
1¼ cup flour
¼ teaspoon sugar
¼ teaspoon salt
⅓ cup plus 3 tablespoons butter-flavor Crisco shortening
2½ tablespoons cold milk

For the filling:
1 tablespoon gelatin
¼ cup pineapple juice
4 eggs, separated
¼ cup sugar
1½ cup sliced cooked fresh pineapple
4 teaspoons lemon juice
¼ teaspoon salt
⅛ teaspoon cream of tartar
½ cup sugar

For the garnish:
Whipped cream
½ cup sliced fresh pineapple
¼ cup unsalted roasted macadamia nut halves
12 candied red cherry halves

No Icing Banana Cake

Yield: 10 to 12 servings

Rose Tagami (Wailuku)

2¼ cups cake flour
½ teaspoon baking powder
¾ teaspoon baking soda
½ teaspoon salt
1 cup banana, mashed
2 bananas, sliced
1 teaspoon vanilla
¼ cup milk or buttermilk
1½ cups sugar
½ cup butter, softened
2 eggs

*T*his recipe won first place in the dessert category at the Maui County Fair in 1954. An active member of the University of Hawai'i Extension Club Home Council, Rose Tagami was elected Woman of the Year in 1952.

Sift flour, baking powder, baking soda, and salt. Add vanilla and milk to mashed banana. Add sugar to butter gradually. Beat until light and creamy. Beat eggs into butter mixture one at a time. Add the sifted ingredients to the butter mixture, one-third at a time. Beat the batter after each addition until it is smooth. Bake the cake in 2 greased 9-inch layer pans in a 350-degree oven for about 30 minutes. Let cool. Place sliced bananas between the layers. Sprinkle with powdered sugar or serve plain with whipped cream.

Guava Tapioca

Yield: 4 to 6 servings

Bonnie Tuell (Makawao)

¼ cup minute tapioca
1 cup sugar
1/8 teaspoon salt
1 cup water
1 tablespoon lemon juice,
    if desired
1 teaspoon lemon rind,
    grated
1 cup unsweetened fresh
    guava juice
½ cup guava shells, thinly
    sliced
Whipped cream (optional)

*G*uava bushes grow profusely in East Maui and supply plentiful fruit. The fruit are versatile and can be used for juice, cobblers, ketchup, pies, cakes, and anything else imaginable. If in Makawao, eat guava the easiest way—stop by Komoda Bakery and pick up a guava malasada.

For this tapioca, use unsweetened fresh guava juice.

To make unsweetened fresh guava juice, put ¼ cup water in blender. Add quartered guavas until the blender is ¾ full. Cover and blend 30 seconds. Strain to remove seeds. Add water until it has the consistency of juice. It will not be the same pink color as commercial juice, as no food coloring is used. Please note: If making guava juice for general consumption, add sugar to taste.

Combine tapioca, sugar, salt and water. Cook slowly over direct heat until tapioca is clear (about 5 minutes). Remove from stove and stir in remaining ingredients, except whipped cream. Pour into individual dishes and chill. Serve with whipped cream, if desired.

Gingered Coconut and Maui Gold Pineapple Tapioca

Hāli'imaile Pineapple Company & Maui Culinary Academy

Yield: 8 servings

Place the cream, coconut milk, sugar, vanilla extract, and grated ginger in a stainless steel saucepan. Bring this cream mixture to a simmer over moderate heat.

Place the egg yolks in a stainless steel bowl. Whisk gently for 1 minute.

Pour the cream mixture over the yolks while whisking constantly.

Return this mixture back to the saucepan. Cook and stir cream mixture over low heat for 3 minutes or until mixture begins to thicken slightly. Be careful not to overcook the cream mixture.

Strain cream mixture into a stainless steel bowl and immediately cool over an ice bath. Once cool, the cream mixture should coat the back of a spoon. Refrigerate cream mixture.

Bring the water to a boil. Stir tapioca into the boiling water and cool until each pearl is clear and opaque.

Pour tapioca into a fine mesh strainer and drain off water. Gently mix the tapioca straight into the cream mixture.

Place one tablespoon of Maui Roasted Pineapple Jam into a small attractive clear glass bowl or glass. Ladle tapioca on top of jam and decorate with fresh whipped cream, a sprig of mint, and a thin wedge of Maui Gold pineapple.

1 cup cream
1 cup unsweetened coconut milk
½ cup granulated sugar
1 teaspoon pure vanilla extract
2 teaspoons freshly grated ginger
6 large egg yolks
1 cup small pearl tapioca
4 cups water for tapioca
1 cup Maui Roasted Pineapple Jam (available at Maui Culinary Academy and other selected sites)

Miscellaneous

Robert Lu'uwai with his boat crew, including his dad and son.

Meat Smoking Sauce

Yield: about 3 cups

Robert Lu'uwai (Waiohuli Kula)

3 cups sugar
3 teaspoons sesame oil
3 cloves garlic, minced
3 cups soy sauce
Pinch of Hawaiian salt
Chopped chili pepper or
    chili pepper water to
    taste

*T*his versatile recipe can be used to smoke or to dry either meat or fish. Fisherman and hunter Robert Lu'uwai has used this recipe on beef, pork, venison, marlin, 'ōpelu, and akule.

Mix together all the ingredients and marinate the meat or fish several hours or overnight. If a smoker is not available, simple dehydrators work well, just give the meat or fish plenty of time to dry. Drying times vary considerably with different models of dehydrators, so it might be a few hours or 24.

Granny Mendonça's Portuguese Sweet Bread

Yield: 7 loaves

Morlee Walters (Waikapū)

6 packages yeast
⅔ cup warm water
2 large potatoes, cooked
    and mashed
⅔ cup evaporated milk
4½ cups sugar (½ cup for
    yeast)
16 cups flour
12 eggs, beaten
2 teaspoons vanilla extract
4 teaspoons salt
½ teaspoon nutmeg
½ pound butter, softened

*T*his old Portuguese recipe makes seven loaves, so that the family would have a loaf to eat every day of the week. When Morlee Walters lived on the mainland, she entered a loaf of this bread in the Oregon Coos County Fair baking competition and won first place.

Mix yeast with water until dissolved. Add potatoes, milk and sugar. Mix and let site for 20 minutes. Dissolve, mix and let sit for 20 minutes. Mix flour, sugar, eggs, vanilla, salt, nutmeg, and butter. Knead half an hour. Let rise 1 hour. Punch down. Let rise 1½ hours. Put in greased pans (7 loaves). Let rise 4 to 5 hours. Bake at 300 degrees for 1 hour.

Liliko'i Jelly

Bonnie Tuell (Makawao)

Yield: about 4 (6-ounce) glasses

½ cup passion fruit juice
3 cups sugar
1 cup water
1 pouch liquid pectin

This jelly, so full of liliko'i flavor and its characteristic tartness, has been used by generations of Maui cooks and as a popular fundraiser for hula hālau. Liliko'i was first grown on Maui and is named for the gulch it was first grown in, Liliko'i Gulch in East Maui.

Mix sugar and water together in a saucepan. Boil for one minute vigorously, stirring. Remove from heat. Stir in liquid pectin. Add liliko'i juice and mix well. Bring to a boil for a few minutes or until it thickens. Skim off foam. Pour jelly into sterilized hot jelly jars and seal with tops.

Cho Jang

Dora Woo Lee and Cynthia Lee Smith (Kula)

Yield: ½ cup

1 heaping tablespoon gochujang (Korean chili paste)
⅓ cup rice vinegar
1½ tablespoons soy sauce
1 tablespoon finely chopped green onion
1 clove minced garlic

This dipping sauce is excellent with sashimi, lettuce wraps, and just about anything. As it is easy to make and keeps well when refrigerated, have it readily available to use as needed. Gochujang is a hot bean paste found in the Asian aisle of supermarkets. It is also good by itself on hot rice in lettuce wraps.

Mix vinegar and soy sauce. Slowly add small amount of this mixture with the gochujang and mix until smooth. Then combine all ingredients.

M. KAWAHARADA RESTAURANT.
KUIAHA.

HOTEL
Hana-Maui
HAWAIIAN ISLANDS

CLUB
RODEO
Steak House

SUB AND MARY MOLINA, Proprietors

MAKAWAO, MAUI, HAWAII

CHOP SUEY HOUSE

GOLDEN
JADE

301 KALAWI DR.   PHONE 244-4050

Aloha Restaurant

LUNCH · DINNER · BAR
PHONE
661-0755

BANYAN
INN & MOTEL
LAHAINA, MAUI,
HAWAII

LUNCH

Carlene's Cafe

SOUPS VEGETABLES & SALADS

PORTUGUESE BEAN SOUP	1.85-2.50
SOUP OF THE DAY	1.85-2.50
SAUTEED EGGPLANT AND ZUCCHINI	4.00
MIXED GREEN SALAD	1.25-2.00
MAUI ONION & TOMATO SALAD	3.00
TUNA SALAD	4.00
FRESH TUNA SALAD (WHEN AVAILABLE)	4.25
POTATO SALAD OR COLE SLAW	.75

SANDWICHES
WITH CARLENE'S BREAD - CHOICE OF POTATO SALAD OR COLE SLAW

GRILLED CHEESE & TUNA	3.50	TURKEY	3.35
GRILLED CHEESE & TOMATO	3.15	BACON, LETTUCE & TOMATO	3.25
GRILLED CHEESE & BACON	3.50	TUNA	3.10
GRILLED CHEESE	2.85	TOFU BURGER	3.15
		TOFU CHEESEBURGER	3.40

HAMBURGERS

BURGER	3.15	CHEESEBURGER	3.65
BURGER WITH SALAD	3.75	CHEESEBURGER WITH SALAD	4.25
HAMBURGER STEAK WITH RICE & SALAD	4.75		

...AKE	1.50

BEER & WINE

...AL WATER	1.25	BUDWEISER	1.25
...RB TEAS	.53	HEINEKEN	1.90
PEKOE TEA	.53	MICHELOB	1.70
MILK	.21-.95	DOS EQUIS	1.90
SOFT DRINKS	.50-.75	WINE BY BOTTLE	

WINE BY THE GLASS

MAIN AND MARKET   242-9003

Restaurants Gone By

Looking back at our favorite restaurants of yesteryear tells us what our community was like and what we were like. Families walked down the street to get an inexpensive meal together. Kids ran around outside after the meal, waiting for their parents. Eating out was a treat, not a habit. Owners and employees greeted their regular customers by name and knew their favorite dishes. Maybe that is why Mauians remember these occasions with such affection, and that the restaurants featured in this chapter are gone but definitely not forgotten.

Maui's restaurants came in different packages. Many paired up with a general store or a drug store. Lucy Goo Pastry Shop sold hamburgers. Hokama's sold electronics and provided full counter service. Entrepreneurship in its many guises adapted to serve the needs of the community.

People from a variety of ethnic groups opened restaurants and ate at restaurants—and not just those associated with their heritage. Yori's served Hawaiian food. Kawaharada's attracted customers with their apple pie. The Spanish name Molina is associated with Portuguese bean soup. Filipino Harold Sambrano cooked up Chinese delicacies at Ming Yuen. And drugstores such as Toda's and Machida's, operated by Japanese pharmacists, offered the most American food of all at their soda fountains. This common situation gives culinary meaning to the concept of Maui as a melting pot.

And, because of it, we have all benefited.

—Gail Ainsworth

Club Rodeo menu, which listed a full filet mignon dinner for $5.25.

CLUB RODEO

Makawao

Salvador (Sub) and Mary Molina established Club Rodeo as a bar and dance floor on the corner of Makawao and Baldwin avenues in 1952. Ten years later, Mary's sister, Ann Tkachenko, added the steak house, an event so momentous for the small cowboy town of Makawao that a parade of 50 horses, floats carrying troupes of musicians (including the family's Molina Orchestra), and cowboy clowns preceded its opening. Later Sub and Mary took over the food operation but didn't change the menu. Customers could count on Monday as prime rib night and every night as Portuguese bean soup night, drawing customers from all over Maui. Some said the soup was the best on Maui, while others declared it was the best in Hawai'i. Upcountry Maui mourned when Club Rodeo closed in the late 1970s.

Enjoy the soup with grilled garlic bread and imagine being back among the cowboys at Club Rodeo.

Restaurants Gone By

Makawao Portuguese Bean Soup

First take a 10-gallon cauldron… Well, that is how Club Rodeo did it, but the home cook can get by with the largest pot available and by adjusting the ingredients. The cook might as well make a large portion because it gets better day by day.

Soak kidney beans overnight and boil the next morning until tender.

Fill a large pot with water to approximately ⅔ level and throw in fresh beef bones. (Club Rodeo had the advantage of using leftover roasted prime rib bones.) Add any vegetable scraps available such as carrot scrapings, onion pieces, celery leaves, and extra lettuce. Let simmer slowly for three hours.

In the meantime, slice 7 links of Portuguese sausage thinly. (Mary Molina preferred Akahi brand, but Akahi is no longer available.) Fry the sausage slowly and remove grease.

Dice 5 pounds of carrots, 5 pounds of celery including the leaves, and 5 pounds of onions. On special family occasions, the Molinas might add chopped Portuguese squash, otherwise known as chayote.

Drain the vegetables and bones from the stock. Put back on the stove and add kidney beans, carrots, celery, and onions. Add 6 ounces of tomato juice for color. Let it simmer very slowly for hours. Take off the burner and let cool. Put in the refrigerator and reheat when needed.

Maui Grand Hotel

Wailuku

Whoever chose the name for this hotel chose wisely. The stately Maui Grand was the best Maui had to offer from the 1930s to its closing in 1961. Duncan Hines, America's famed authority on where to stay and where to eat, listed the Maui Grand Hotel in his selective guides throughout the 1950s. Wailuku reigned as the center of travel activity on Maui at that time. The hotel was located on the corner of Main and Church streets, now occupied by a gas station. Maui Cookery by Frances Wadsworth, published in 1944, printed a recipe from the Maui Grand Hotel provided by Mrs. E. J. Walsh, the co-owner and manager.

Filipino community banquet at the Maui Grand Hotel.

Maui Grand Hotel Cheesecake

Yield: 10 to 12 servings

6 oz. Zwieback (or graham crackers)
1 cup sugar
1 teaspoon cinnamon
½ cup chopped walnuts
5 ounces melted butter
4 eggs
2 cups sugar
½ teaspoon salt
½ lemon, both juice and zest
½ cup vanilla extract
½ pint cream
1½ pounds cottage cheese (today's cook would use ricotta)
¼ cup flour

Roll Zwieback or graham crackers to a fine texture. Mix with 1 cup of sugar, cinnamon, nuts, and melted butter. Set aside 1 cup of crumb mixture to sprinkle on top. Butter a 9-inch pan. Spread and press crumb mixture on bottom and sides of pan. Beat eggs with remaining sugar until light. Add salt, lemon and vanilla. Blend cream into egg mixture. Add cheese and flour and mix well. Strain and force through sieve. Stir until smooth. Pour into springform pan and cover with remaining crumb mixture. Bake 1 hour at 350 degrees. Turn heat off, open door and let cool in oven for 1 hour.

Hotel Hana Maui

Hāna

*S*tarting out as Hotel Hana Ranch in 1947, the Hotel Hana Maui has had multiple owners, varied restaurants, and menus as diverse as the people who came to Hāna from around the world. The hotel hired local chefs who provided regularly-scheduled lū'aus, as well as breakfast, lunch, and dinner. The food at the hotel restaurant fed Roy Rogers and Dale Evans, Susan Hayward, Clark Gable, and many more celebrities and world leaders. The restaurant, personifying Hawaiian hospitality, offered an extra helping to anyone who asked for it.

One particular celebrity as well as gourmet, Vincent Price of horror movie fame, published a cookbook in 1965 that provided recipes of "famous specialties of the world's foremost restaurants adapted for the American kitchen." Hotel Hana Maui was in elite company and the only restaurant from Hawai'i included. Mr. Price called the following recipe "most unusual, most delicious." He liked to serve it in thin slices with a cup of coffee at any time of the night or day.

While enjoying this, the realization may hit that anyone can eat like a celebrity.

Hotel Hana Maui menu from the 1960s.

Pineapple Nut Bread

Preheat oven to 350 degrees. Butter two 1-pound loaf pans. Sift together the measured flour, baking powder, baking soda, and salt. Stir in macadamia nuts. In a separate bowl, cream butter and sugar. Beat in eggs and continue to beat until mixture is smooth. Stir in half the flour-nut mixture. Stir in 2 cups crushed pineapple and juice. Stir in the remaining flour-nut mixture, and stir until well blended. Divide batter into the prepared pans. Combine sugar and cinnamon. Sprinkle half the sugar-cinnamon mixture over batter in each pan and bake for 50 to 60 minutes, or until bread tests done. Let cool for 5 minutes, then turn out on cake rack to cool.

Yield: 2 (1-pound) loaves

3½ cups sifted flour
4 teaspoons baking powder
½ teaspoon baking soda
1 teaspoon salt
1½ cups coarsely chopped macadamia nuts
6 tablespoons of butter, softened
1½ cups light brown sugar, firmly packed
2 eggs
2 cups crushed pineapple with juice
4 tablespoons sugar
1 teaspoon cinnamon

Aloha Restaurant

Kahului

Aloha Restaurant sign at its location on Pu'unēnē Avenue, Kahului.

Top: Preparing pigs to go into the imu at Aloha Restaurant. Bottom: Alexander DePonte, son of Aloha Restaurant's founders, is at the back of the photo.

From World War II to the 1980s, the DePonte family fed tens of thousands of people, both locals and visitors. Manuel DePonte Sr., with the Hawaiian knowledge of his Hāna-born wife, Aggie Aikau DePonte, started catering lū'au for servicemen during the war and established the first Aloha Restaurant on Ka'ahumanu Avenue near today's hotel row. Aloha Restaurant moved to Pu'unēnē Avenue in 1958, migrating to its final site ten years later, across from the current Kahului Post Office. The restaurant's specialty was Hawaiian food, and lots of it. They could cook up to 16 pigs at one time in an imu located behind the restaurant and catered 200 lū'au a year. In the early days, if a large event needed a caterer, Aloha was it. Aloha Restaurant catered events for Richard Nixon and Jesse Kuhaulua, as well as for the openings of the Wailea Shopping Center and the Hyatt Regency. On site, Aloha Restaurant offered Hawaiian, Japanese, and American food in the front of the restaurant and banquet facilities for 600 in the back, which was called the Lū'au House. Maui lost a landmark eatery when Aloha Restaurant closed.

Former manager Ruth DePonte could not provide any detailed recipes as they cooked in huge quantities, but did share some secrets to one of their specialties, tripe stew, which she learned from her mother-in-law, who cooked it in the old Hawaiian way.

Tripe Stew

Clean thoroughly and then wipe the tripe with lemon juice to whiten it before cooking, if necessary. (Most tripe available today has been pre-cleaned.) Boil the tripe for several hours until soft. (The tripe in markets today is often pre-cooked and requires less cooking time.) Add onions, garlic, tomato sauce, salt, and pepper, and simmer until done. Ruth warns us not to stretch out the dish by adding too many vegetables compared to the tripe. It just wouldn't be as good as Aloha Restaurant made it.

BANYAN INN

Lahaina

George and Ruth Tan started in business across from the historic Lahaina banyan in the late 1930s with a skating rink and a snack bar, which became popular with military men crowding Lahaina during World War II. Shortly thereafter they built the Banyan Inn, Lahaina's first steak house, which retained its popularity for decades. The open-air building, with walls of flowers, shrubs, and trees provided a comfortable Hawaiian atmosphere, and its food drew people from far parts of the island until its closing in the mid-1960s.

SIZZLING STEAK

Their specialty was sizzling steak, where T-bone, Porterhouse, and New York steaks from Pioneer Mill beef were grilled to the point of being slightly underdone. The chef heated an aluminum platter to a high heat and placed a rare steak on the platter to complete the cooking process. The steak would arrive on the table as medium rare, just as the customer ordered.

The person who wielded this magic for 40 years was chef Lorraine Iwamura Fujiyama, who was also the restaurant's baker, famous for her homemade breads and picture-perfect pies. Lorraine said the dessert most in-demand was the blueberry cream cheese pie, which they sold for 35 cents a slice, and she has graciously shared the recipe.

A vintage ashtray, and the Banyan Inn menu, which depicts Lahaina's landmark tree.

The Maui community lost a landmark restaurant when the Banyan Inn closed in 1986. Fortunately, a grandson of George and Ruth Tan still serves blueberry cream cheese tartlets at his Nāpili restaurant, Mama's Ribs & Rotisserie. And the recipe is here at hand.

Blueberry Cream Cheese Pie

In a small bowl, combine whipping cream with vanilla. Using hand mixer, whip until firm. Set aside in refrigerator.

In a medium bowl, combine cream cheese with sugar and mix until light.

Add whipping cream mixture and mix or fold together. Pour into a cooled baked pie crust. Top with blueberry filling. Refrigerate for a minimum of 2 hours before serving.

1 cup (half pint) whipping cream

½ teaspoon vanilla extract

1 (8-ounce) block of cream cheese (none of that fat-free stuff)

½ cup powdered sugar

1 (21-ounce) can Comstock or other blueberry filling

1 (8¾-inch) prepared pie crust (baked and cooled)

Left: Kitchen staff and sommelier Johnny Valera at the Bay Club.

Right: Tables awaiting guests at the luxurious Bay Club.

THE BAY CLUB

Kapalua

The Kapalua Bay Hotel and its gourmet restaurant the Bay Club oozed elegance, but unlike many other expensive resorts, it was understated elegance. The Bay Club was located in the most beautiful location at Kapalua on "The Point," where diners feasted on both fabulous food and indescribable sunsets. At lunch the Bay Club was famous for its small but unique buffet, which included plentiful sashimi, popular with the local crowd. The service was exceptional every day of the week but, on special occasions, servers carved everything tableside, whether it was duck, fish, or meat. The Bay Club had an exceptional wine list, which boasted several high-end wines. The restaurant has been called the most romantic setting in all of Hawai'i, where lovers had an open-air and expansive view of Kapalua Bay and Moloka'i. Built in 1977 as a private club, it opened to the public in 1978 and closed in 2006.

Chef Mark Whitehead has kindly provided us with a recipe for his signature dish from the Bay Club. The only ingredient missing is the view.

Seared 'Ahi Tartare with Pickled Shiitake Mushrooms

Trim and cut the 'ahi into ¼-inch cubes. Mix the oils, capers, chili paste, parsley and green onions together. Season the 'ahi with salt. Add the oil mixture to the 'ahi and stir it together. Heat a sauté pan on medium heat on the stove. Add a tablespoon of olive oil to the pan. Place a 3-inch round mold into the sauté pan. (This readily-available mold is used to hold the cake together.) Spoon 3 ounces of the 'ahi mixture into the mold and sear until golden brown. Flip the mold over and sear on the opposite side. Be sure not to overcook it as the goal is to keep the inside rare. Remove the 'ahi from the mold and place in the middle of the plate. Garnish with ogo and pickled mushrooms.

Yield: 4 cakes

1 (12-ounce) 'ahi filet
1 tablespoon sesame oil
2 tablespoon olive oil
2 tablespoons capers
1 teaspoon Thai chili paste
¼ cup parsley (optional)
½ cup green onions, minced
Hawaiian salt to taste
Ogo, chopped (optional)
3 tablespoons Pickled Mushroom Salsa (recipe follows)

Pickled Mushroom Salsa

Heat oils in a sauté pan. Add shallots, garlic, green onions, and ginger; sauté until tender. Add the shiitake and toss in the oil. Add to the same pan the soy sauce, sake, vinegar, wine and chili paste and make sure all solids and liquids are dissolved. Bring to a simmer and reduce until liquid absorbs into the mushrooms. Season to taste with salt and pepper.

Yield: about ½ cup

1 tablespoon sesame oil
1 tablespoon olive oil
1 shallot, minced (or Maui onion)
1 clove of garlic, minced
½ cup green onions, sliced
1 teaspoon ginger, minced
1 pound shiitake mushrooms, sliced
1 tablespoon soy sauce
1 tablespoon sake
2 tablespoons rice wine vinegar
1 tablespoons white wine
1 teaspoon Thai chili paste
Salt and pepper to taste

Ming Yuen

Kahului

Before Ming Yuen opened in the early 1980s, Chinese food on Maui meant Cantonese food. Ming Yuen served many Cantonese dishes, but also introduced the spicier Schezuan style of cooking from Northern China. Some of the Schezuan dishes the restaurant was noted for were Mongolian beef, hot-and-sour soup, kung pao chicken, and Schezuan eggplant.

Ming Yuen, a large and formal restaurant by Maui standards, took reservations and decorated with Chinese antiques. On Chinese New Year, the restaurant served a 10-course banquet complete with firecrackers, which startled the crowd with the enormity of the display. Ming Yuen occupied the building on Alamaha Street that now houses Hawaiian One Carpets until it closed in the mid-1990s. Although Mauians miss Ming Yuen, they can now reminisce with a bowl of their specialty eggplant, the recipe recalled by part-owner and chef Harold Sambrano.

Harold Sambrano's Famous Schezuan Eggplant

Yield: 4 servings

1 eggplant, 1- to 1½-pound
½ teaspoon ginger, minced
1 teaspoon garlic, minced
3 tablespoons sugar
3 tablespoon light soy sauce
2 teaspoons dark soy sauce
1 tablespoon sherry
2 tablespoons white vinegar
1 teaspoon do ban jiang
   (chili bean paste)
1 heaping teaspoon
   cornstarch
¾ cup chicken stock
1 teaspoon sesame oil
1 green onion, finely sliced
1 red jalapeño pepper,
   finely sliced

Oil for deep-frying

Peel eggplant, cut in half horizontally. Cut each piece into sticks approximately 1 inch x 1 inch x 3½ inch. Deep-fry sticks until brown and tender. Place on paper towels to drain some of the oil.

In a small bowl, mix ingredients to make the sauce: ginger, garlic, sugar, light and dark soy, sherry and vinegar, do ban jiang, cornstarch and chicken stock.

Heat wok or large sauté pan. Add cooked eggplant and all of the sauce mixture. Bring to a boil until the sauce thickens.

Place on a serving platter or bowl. Add sesame oil, green onion, and jalapeño pepper.

Ming Yuen's in-demand Schezuan eggplant.

TODA DRUG STORE

Kahului

Umeyo and Robert Toda opened their drug store in 1929, and their son Takashi and his wife Myrtle took over in the later years. In 1940, the Kahului branch of Toda Drug Store remodeled and proudly announced, "The most important feature of the store is the modernistic Liquid Carbonic stainless-steel soda fountain and lunch counter which has been installed. Nine blue-padded swivel stools of the comfortable variety have been installed at the fountain, which is carried out in walnut, royal blue and stainless steel." Toda's was certainly not the only soda fountain on Maui, but it was considered the finest of its time and it lasted the longest. In 1955, when Toda Drug moved to the new Kahului Shopping Center, it continued its counter service and took care of a large number of dedicated customers until it closed in 1992.

It was known for the quality of its hamburgers, milk shakes, sundaes, and coffee. And they sold POG way before it became trendy. The lunch counter snaked toward the back of the store and was filled with children spinning around on the stools and adults drinking coffee, smoking and reading, which was made easy by magazines and newspapers available in a rack close to the counter. Sitting at a counter also promoted socializing as, even if someone was a newcomer, he or she ended up talking to the person at the next stool.

Not all hamburgers are alike, and Toda's hamburgers were true originals.

From left, Takashi Toda, Namiye Nakamura, Toshiko Nakamura, Betty Oura, Charlotte Orikasa, Betsy Yoshida, May Kong, Ethel Tanaka, Umeyo Toda, Robert S. Toda, and Lillian Sanehira, ca. 1956.

Toda Drug Hamburgers

Mix all ingredients together. Form into patties and fry. Grill bun to warm; spread with mayonnaise, mustard and/or ketchup. Serve with lettuce and tomato. Sliced onion is optional.

Yield: 4 servings

1 pound lean ground beef
1½ teaspoons salt
1½ teaspoons sugar
1½ teaspoons vinegar
1½ teaspoons soy sauce
1½ teaspoons
  Worcestershire sauce
1 egg
1 cup chopped onion
1 cup grated potato

CARLENE'S CAFÉ

Wailuku

LUNCH

Carlene's Café

SOUPS VEGETABLES & SALADS

PORTUGUESE BEAN SOUP	1.85-2.50
SOUP OF THE DAY	1.85-2.50
SAUTEED EGGPLANT AND ZUCCHINI	4.00
MIXED GREEN SALAD	1.25-2.00
MAUI ONION & TOMATO SALAD	3.00
TUNA SALAD	4.00
FRESH TUNA SALAD (WHEN AVAILABLE)	4.25
POTATO SALAD OR COLE SLAW	.75

SANDWICHES
WITH CARLENE'S BREAD - CHOICE OF POTATO SALAD OR COLE SLAW

GRILLED CHEESE & TUNA	3.50	TURKEY	3.35
GRILLED CHEESE & TOMATO	3.15	BACON, LETTUCE & TOMATO	3.25
GRILLED CHEESE & BACON	3.20	TUNA	3.10
GRILLED CHEESE	2.85	TOFU BURGER	3.15
TOFU CHEESEBURGER	3.40		

HAMBURGERS

HAMBURGER	3.15	CHEESEBURGER	3.65
HAMBURGER WITH SALAD	3.75	CHEESEBURGER WITH SALAD	4.25
HAMBURGER STEAK WITH RICE & SALAD			4.75

DESSERTS

HOMEMADE PIE	1.50	HOMEMADE CAKE	1.50
ICE CREAM			1.25

BEVERAGES

COFFEE	.53
COFFEE REFILL	.20
HERB TEAS	.53
PEKOE TEA	.53
MILK	.53-.75
SOFT DRINKS	.53-.75

BEER & WINE

MINERAL WATER	1.25
BUDWEISER	1.25
HEINEKEN	1.90
MICHELOB	1.70
DOS EQUIS	1.90
WINE BY BOTTLE	
WINE BY THE GLASS	2.00

MAIN AND MARKET STREET • WAILUKU, MAUI, HAWAII • TELEPHONE (808) 242-9003

Carlene's menu, showing 1970s-1980s prices.

When Carlene's Café opened on the corner of Main and Market in Wailuku in the late 1970s, it stood out among the local restaurants in town. Owner Carlene Carrasco was straight from the mainland and had never run a restaurant, though she was an experienced baker and had worked for catering companies. She sought and received advice from many friendly Mauians, such as Winona Rogers of Rogers' Meat Market, who taught her about cuts of meat and gave her recipes. However, her naiveté occasionally led to problems. Her accountant told her she had to have local dishes, so she cooked her first pot of Portuguese bean soup the day before she opened and then had to throw it out as it had fermented. Another challenge turned to an opportunity when, not realizing how big a tuna is, she ordered one from two Māʻalaea fishermen. Overwhelmed with fish, she invented tuna burgers. She was a quick learner, an experienced cook, and hired good staff, and the restaurant prospered. Carlene's was the first lunch restaurant on Maui that didn't have a standard hamburger/plate lunch menu. She became known for her herb bread, which was often used to make tuna melts. We are fortunate Carlene has shared her recipe for herb bread and Winona Rogers's short rib recipe with us, so that they can outlive her restaurant, which closed in the early 1980s.

Three Delectable Loaves of Carlene's Herb Bread

Put yeast in warm, but not hot, water with honey. Honey varies in taste so use honey that is not too strong but adds sweetness to the bread. Let stand for 5 minutes and be sure the yeast is foamy and smells like bread. That proves that the yeast is active.

In a food processor, blend mixture ingredients well. Combine this mixture with the yeast in a large mixing bowl and stir. Begin to add approximately 14 cups of flour. (Flours are variable.) Keep adding flour until the dough cleans the side of the bowl and forms a cohesive mass. Knead on a floured flat surface about ten minutes until dough is smooth and elastic. Let rise for 1 to 2 hours in a covered oiled bowl until doubled in volume and, if poked, the impression remains in the dough. Preheat oven to 350 degrees. Punch down, shape into desired loaves and place in loaf pans. Let rise a second time. Bake for 35 to 40 minutes. Glaze with a mixture of egg yolk and water during the last 5 minutes of baking.

4½ tablespoons yeast
4½ tablespoons warm water (not hot)
½ cup honey

Mixture:
⅜ cup (¼ cup plus 2 tablespoons) canola or safflower oil
2½ tablespoons salt
2 tablespoons dried oregano
1½ tablespoons dried dill weed
½ medium-sized onion
1 tablespoon dried dill seed
2 cloves garlic
2 tablespoons dried basil
½ cup dried parsley
2 tablespoons dried marjoram

14 cups flour
2 egg yolks, beaten
¼ cup water

Winona Rogers's Waikapū Short Ribs

Cut meat into serving pieces. Flour and salt individual pieces and put into baking pan. Place slices of onion on top, cover with aluminum foil and bake in a 350 degree oven for 1½ hours. Pour off grease and add sauce. Lower heat to 300 degrees, and bake another 45 minutes until the meat is tender but not falling off the bone. Let cool in refrigerator overnight and remove any remaining grease the next day. To reheat for eating, heat oven to 350 degrees and bake for 25 to 30 minutes. Excellent as a plate lunch with rice.

To make the barbecue sauce, combine all the ingredients.

Serves 24 to 26

5 pounds short ribs
Flour and salt for dredging
1 onion sliced

For the barbecue sauce:
¾ cup Heinz ketchup
¾ cup water
½ cup sugar (optional)
4 tablespoons soy sauce
2 tablespoons apple cider vinegar
2 tablespoons Worcestershire sauce
a little crushed red pepper flakes (to taste)

KAWAHARADA'S

Ku'iaha, Ha'ikū

Owners Makizo and Harumi Kawaharada, Mr. Kawaharada, in a business suit, and Mrs. Kawaharada holding a baby. The three women on the right are restaurant workers. The other children are all Kawaharadas, the first seven of ten.

Makizo Kawaharada opened his business in 1929, making his restaurant one of the longest lasting in Maui history, closing in the mid-1990s. Kawaharada's, located directly across from the Libby, McNeill and Libby Pa'uwela cannery, catered to a bustling pineapple plantation district. But the restaurant's appeal reached far beyond Ha'ikū. A group of Kahului businessmen traveled each and every Wednesday to Kawaharada's for saimin and pie. How could one have Kawaharada saimin without Kawaharada pie, particularly apple pie? In fact, the appeal of saimin and pie was so strong that some customers ate them at the same time.

For many years matriarch Harumi Kawaharada was a one-woman noodle- and pie-maker. But the demand became too great and, though she still made the homemade noodles, she had to pass on the pie-making to others. The restaurant ran mostly with family labor. All ten children worked at one time or another at the restaurant and also put time in as cannery workers.

Kawaharada's was a no-frills restaurant with customers sitting on benches at long tables. But it was far from gloomy, as it served as a socializing center for many from miles around. Maui residents still mourn the loss of Kawaharada's saimin, the variety of luscious pies and the old-fashioned doughnuts made and served in the morning.

GOLDEN JADE CHOP SUEY HOUSE

Wailuku

Albert and Shirley Chee opened Golden Jade in Wailuku close to the armory and ran their successful restaurant over the years with the help of relatives in both the Chee and Tom families, particularly Annie Tom, the head cook, and her son, Wallace, who took over when she retired. Golden Jade celebrated their first anniversary in 1957 by holding a drawing that offered as first prize a nine-course Chinese dinner for six. Whoever won that prize was lucky indeed, as Golden Jade offered an extensive menu of delicious Chinese food. Golden Jade wasn't the only Chinese restaurant in town, but it was considered by many to be the best.

One of their specialties was stuffed duck, which customers had to order one day ahead. Another favorite was take-out Chinese-style turkey. Anyone could order this throughout the year but, of course, Thanksgiving was the usual time. Customers brought their own whole turkey in their own pot and it would return roasted, transformed in taste, and cut into small pieces the Chinese way. Those waiting for their cooked turkey would wait outside the restaurant talking story with other eager eaters until their bird was ready. The aroma seeping from the turkey lingers fondly in the culinary memory of many Mauians.

A fan put her experience this way, "My friends and I had more than one favorite on the menu at Golden Jade, but we would almost always order the same thing—small bowls of crispy gau gee mein with vegetables. A small bowl was just right and the price fit our budgets. I especially liked dipping my crispy gau gee into the noodle gravy while consuming the vegetables and curly wheat noodles. The combination of crispy and salty won ton dipped into heavenly sweetened brown gravy was addicting. If Golden Jade still served crispy gau gee mein today, I'd be a blimp."

Golden Jade sought to offer quality, value, and hospitality. A menu from the 1960s promised "Your money's worth in exquisite cuisine," and greeted their patrons with "Thank you for coming. Make yourselves feel at home." Customers will testify that Golden Jade continued to fulfill these promises until they closed in the mid-1990s.

Golden Jade menu, with a photo of the well-known Wailuku restaurant.

Kitada's Kau Kau Korner

Makawao

"Breakfast, lunch and aloha in beautiful downtown Makawao" promised the sign at the Upcountry town's much-beloved restaurant. Ethel Kitada Hotema felt the key to Kitada's success and longevity was just that, the many friends the family acquired though the years. Takeshi and Suteko Kitada opened Kitada's as a store and restaurant in 1947, selling not just groceries, but fishing supplies, clothing, and jewelry. The two had met through shinpai, an arranged marriage, and formed a long and happy partnership in both life and business.

The Kitadas moved into the same humble wood structure that exists today, which changed very little throughout its life as a restaurant, still housing the original tables and benches. That can be said of most of their menu as well. Until they closed in 2007, they served the same bestselling chop steak, hekka, and hamburger steak as they did in the 1940s.

A steady stream of regular customers came to talk story, while eating saimin or a hefty but inexpensive plate lunch accompanied by salted cabbage, macaroni salad, and two scoops of rice. Ethel Hotema, when asked for a mac salad recipe to remember Kitada's by, said she just couldn't do it. How could she? "You just boil the noodles, throw in the mayonnaise, carrots, salt and pepper. If it tastes right, it is done."

Mayor Hannibal Tavares and Suteko Kitada celebrating at Takeshi Kitada's annual birthday bash at the restaurant, with Komoda Bakery cake, of course.

Suteko Kitada, whom everyone called Mrs. Kitada, was the queen of Makawao, some said. She had a kolohe, flirtatious manner which so charmed Frank DeLima that he would visit regularly to sing to her in Japanese. Mr. Kitada, also fun-loving, often broke out his abacus to tote up a bill, shifting beads for an extended time to come up with $1.90 for a plate lunch and a soda. His serious demeanor belied the fact that he had just put on a show to impress a newcomer.

Kitada's was the type of place where customers poured coffee, picked soda out of the cooler, and grabbed a cloth if the table needed wiping. Being in Kitada's felt comfortable. That was why it was a shock when the family announced their closing in 2007. It would take too much money to renovate the old building to meet current standards. A regular customer who had been doing the restaurant's plumbing for free, gathered a group of contractors to offer discounted services, and customers offered to donate money. But to no avail. Kitada's time had come.

The family held a close-out sale which drew hundreds of customers. People snaked down Baldwin Avenue to have the chance to buy canned tomatoes, pitchers, buckets, T-shirts, and a few items that had been stored for decades. Portraits of George Washington and Abraham Lincoln, sold by the Kitadas to their Japanese neighbors who wanted to bolster their claim on patriotism went like hotcakes. And in a poignant illustration of aloha to the community, each and every customer received a free chop steak plate lunch.

PINEAPPLE HILL

Honolua/Kapalua

West Maui enjoyed a surge of population in the early sixties due to the establishment of Kā'anapali as a tourist destination. No longer a sleepy plantation town, Lahaina rapidly became fashionable. And north of Kā'anapali, Nāpili was beginning to bloom.

In 1963, mainland residents Alfred and Mary Jane Holmes bought the charming and historic Fleming home above Nāpili Bay and opened the doors as a restaurant named Pineapple Hill. David Fleming Sr., pineapple plantation manager and well-known agricultural expert, had planted Norfolk pine trees along the mile-long driveway and exotic landscaping on the property. Restaurant guests could enjoy a cocktail on a manicured lawn near a splashing fountain. The elevation afforded a lofty setting for sunset viewing, with a panorama of Lahaina Roads and Moloka'i. And beyond the lawn lay neat rows of pineapple, still flourishing on the West Side.

In the 1980s, Pineapple Hill was still a welcome bit of relaxed old Hawai'i. The circular drive bisected a lush garden of tropical plants and parrots in cages. Patrons could drop off their friends in front of the veranda steps, flanked on both sides by large river rock pillars. The main dining room was one big homey room, furnished to guarantee quiet, so that guests could have spirited conversations over a good meal.

The specialties of the house in its early days were Chicken Pineapple Hill, an original recipe of oven-roasted chicken served in a pineapple boat, and Fresh Maui Turtle Steak. Jerrold and Eileen McDonald then bought the restaurant and Pineapple Hill became part of the Buzz's family of restaurants.

Picturesque Pineapple Hill, with its circular drive and line of Norfolk pine trees.

Shrimp Tahitian became a specialty, made by butterflying the shrimp, basting them with vermouth, and sprinkling them with seasonings and Parmesan cheese before grilling or baking. What made the shrimp dishes particularly special was that the shrimp were flown in from the McDonald family shrimp farm in New Caledonia. The last remaining member of that family of restaurants, Buzz's Wharf in Ma'alaea, has been open since 1966 and still makes Shrimp Tahitian in much the same way Pineapple Hill did. It is their signature dish.

Sadly, Pineapple Hill closed their doors in the 1990s, and the historic home is gone.

PICNICS

Pā'ia

A painting of Picnics by E. Flotte (1985)

Picnics opened in 1979 in the location of the former well-known Pā'ia business, Machida Drugs. On moving into the building, Picnics' owner Hugh Starr found Machida's old soda fountain. Unfortunately, the soda fountain had to go, as Pā'ia was transforming into a new community and was ready for a new style of eatery.

Hugh Starr describes his former business as a "fresh fast food" counter-service restaurant. They baked sandwich buns fresh daily onsite, along with breakfast pastries such as croissant, scones, and Danish. Ahead of their time, they used home-made organic beef for their hamburgers (the meat obtained from independent rancher Bill Eby); roasted all the sandwich meats at the restaurant; and used long-time Kula vegetable farmer, Norman Choda's, fresh Mānoa leaf lettuce, to cite a few examples. And Picnics brought espresso coffee to Pā'ia.

Most famous of all Picnics' offerings, the Spinach Nut Burger was a grilled spinach-peanut-onion patty, with Cheddar cheese, lettuce, tomato, and sprouts, on a butter-basted, grilled fresh whole wheat bun with sauce. Many repeat visitors would say they would come straight from the airport to Picnics for a Spinach Nut Burger before they even drove to their hotel.

Local residents comprised about half of Picnics' business, and visitors usually traveling to Hāna comprised the other half. Hours were typically 6:30 AM to 2 PM daily. Picnics and the windsurf craze arose at the same point in Pā'ia's history, so most of the famous ocean sports women and men would hit Picnics after the day's water session at nearby Ho'okipa or other North Shore spots.

Hugh Starr sold both the building and the business in 1994 and Picnics continued on in name for about 10 years. After that, Mambo Café opened in the location. Some years after opening, Mambo Café has re-posted the name Picnics below their name and offers picnic lunches for visitors to Hāna. Picnics just refuses to die.

I Remember When ...

Vineyard Chop Suey was owned by the Dang family in Wailuku. To many in Central Maui, saying "we go eat Chinese tonight" was the same as saying, "we go Vineyard Chop Suey." The screen door led to the back room where people had large parties, weddings, and family get-togethers. There was a long driveway alongside the restaurant where kids would run around and play after dinner while the adults stayed inside and talked story.

A loyal fan reminisces, "Our family would often eat at **Vineyard Chop Suey** in Wailuku. Though we ordered different items on the menu for the main part of our meal, we always ordered the same thing to start the meal—the abalone soup. The abalone—real abalone, not like today—came in real chunks in a clear broth with Chinese cabbage. I would give anything to have that recipe today."

Nothing was more "Maui" than how French fries were eaten at **Dairy Queen.** Mauians routinely loaded up both ketchup and mustard on their fries. The mustard wasn't plain mustard, but a mixture of mustard, mayonnaise, and a little relish. Ambrosia to a Mauian. A Coke and French fries cost 25 cents in the 1960s and if a lucky person had $1, he or she could splurge and take home 11 Dilly Bars.

Patrons of the **Yamamoto Store** fountain in Lahaina said they had the best shave ice in town and others praised their hamburgers. While enjoying the cool syrupy treat or a juicy burger, a hungry fisherman could also check out the latest in fishing gear, or thousands of other items offered at the store.

Near-legendary restaurant and store owner Bill Azeka sold Maui's "sweet meat," ribs in marinade lauded as the best local people ever tasted. For decades he sold ribs out of his Kīhei **Azeka's** store, plus extremely popular boiled peanuts and shaved ice. While picking up the ribs, the kids could go out back and watch the monkeys kept in a cage. Then when the store closed, Mr. Azeka opened **Azeka's Ribs and Snack Shop.** If anyone spent beach time down in Kīhei, and everyone did, the smell of barbecuing **Azeka's** ribs permeated the air. A truly sweet memory.

Yamamoto Store, whose fountain relieved those suffering from the heat in Lahaina.

Couldn't afford to go out to eat? No problem! Get burlap bags and go pick liliko'i or guava. Haleakalā Dairy paid cash for the fruit that went into POG. East Maui residents could accumulate enough money to feed the family at their favorite restaurant. And then there was barter. A bag of ogo could get a manju or a lunch at **Wing Sing** in Wailuku.

In 1963 **Cupies** began in Kahului as an A&W Root Beer stand. Customers could drive their car in, carhops would come out to take orders and then hook the trays on windows when orders came up. Families would arrive with kids in pajamas and mom in hair rollers but, eh, who cared? No one had to get out of the car.

Wing Sing on Lower Main Street holds the hearts of many. The restaurant made their own noodles, was a popular place to eat after going to the beach, and even had a dish called the Eddie Tam special, named after the popular Chairman of the Board of Supervisors.

Masa and Charlene Hokama, flanked by customers in front of their television store/fountain service.

Though many think of **Hokama's** as a Wailuku music or television store, owner Masa Hokama also opened a counter service restaurant upstairs, with Masa himself flipping burgers. Masa spent too much time talking to the restaurant customers, so his counter service came to a close. One day years later, a naïve customer went upstairs to get lunch, and found Masa still up there sitting on the same counter talking to someone. Masa, being a very friendly man, offered the stranger a cup of coffee.

Way before Lahaina became a tourist mecca, the town was just another local gathering place. If someone wanted saimin, he or she could send the nearest child down to a small Japanese restaurant with a bento container. The child would ask to have it filled up with saimin and then head home.

Mauians, Americans all, loved hamburgers. Each person had their favorite when it came to the classic sandwich. Those from Wailuku and Kahului raved about the **Lucy Goo Pastry Shop** version, saying that it broke da mouth. Some fans called it the Gooburger. But what about **Wimpy's** in Pā'ia? Pā'ia residents swore by **Wimpy's** burgers. And **Toda Drugs** in Kahului? Local favorites all.

Upcountry folk insisted that **Bullock's** Moonburger was the best. **Bullock's** was founded in the 1960s by Paul and Hazel Elkins, who used ground sirloin from Tony DeCoite's slaughter house and vegetables from local farmers. In season, avocados and mangoes came from trees on the property. Bullock's was known, not just for its Moonburger, but for its mango and guava milkshakes, avocado-studded salads, weak coffee, and conviviality. But why was it called a Moonburger? Various explanations circulate, but one dependable source states, "The two-patty, five-napkin Moonburger was invented by Hazel to stuff the mouth of an annoyingly vociferous customer while others wanted to watch the first man on the moon telecast." Despite closing in 1993, the **Bullock's** sign remains today at the same site, still proclaiming itself "The Home of the Moonburger."

Bullock's, forever remembered as the home of the Moonburger.

Bullock's in Pukalani was the type of restaurant even in the 1970s where the same person took the lunch order, cooked the meal, served the customer, and then took the money. In the 1950s and 1960s there were many restaurants on Maui that could boast the same one-on-one service.

Hew Store, which started as a Pā'ia store and restaurant in 1909, made their own saimin noodles and broth and sold it for 5 cents a bowl. A long-lived and much-loved restaurant, **Hew Store** sold the same size saimin in 1980 for 90 cents. What is the cost now?

In 1980, Violet Hew Zane, a member of the family that owned **Hew Store and Restaurant** in Pā'ia, recalled, "All different nationalities used to come to the store. Especially, the restaurant...They all liked saimin—the home-made saimin. They just loved my parents' apple pies and coconut pies, home-made French bread."

Iwaishi Store of Makawao evolved from a store and restaurant into being just a restaurant in the 1970s. They offered counter service for breakfast and lunch, and quickly gained fame for their tofu omelet, which appealed to local and haole alike.

Anyone who lived in Upcountry or East Maui prior to the 1980s could not forget **Wimpy's Corner**, because it was situated on the busy corner of Baldwin and Hāna highways. In fact, it is still considered a geographical place name to kamaʻāina, as in "You go down Baldwin, turn left at Wimpy's Corner, and it is the third shop on the right." As might be guessed, **Wimpy's Corner** made excellent hamburgers, but also served great saimin, both favorites of Pāʻia resident Kealiʻi Reichel, Maui's music star and kumu hula.

The introduction of Schezuan cooking to Maui did pose a danger. One time at **Ming Yuen**, a customer bit into one of the hot peppers meant for only seasoning, not eating, causing his voice to rise by an octave throughout his lunch.

Maui restaurants that opened up after 10:00 were rare in the 1960s. **Yama's** on Lower Main Street was one and **Gate 21** at the airport another. Politicians tended to hang out at **Yama's** after long government sessions, so *Maui News* reporters knew where to find them.

Liberty Café, a long-standing Pāʻia eatery.

Maui's new Kahului Airport, opened in 1966, included a three-level restaurant named **Gate 21**. For the first ten years, Webb Beggs ran **Gate 21**, where night owls could get a burger and a beer. The bar was at the top level, the second level had food, and the bottom level had an unobstructed view of the planes taking off and landing. Free access to the terminal, plus free parking, made **Gate 21** a popular alternative to Kahului and Wailuku eateries.

Mr. and Mrs. Juichi Kurasaki owned a popular restaurant in the 1960s called **Kurasaki's Café**. The café drew customers from nearby Aloha Lanes and throughout central Maui. Their claims to fame were their late hours, steak dinners, and legions of fans. The Kurasakis had previously run **Liberty Café** in Pāʻia.

Naokee's in Wailuku served steak, more steak and even more steak. They also offered free pūpūs to customers who ordered a drink. A drinker was lucky if seared ʻahi showed up on the table.

Liberty Restaurant on Front Street in Lahaina was known for an oddly-named, but wildly popular dish called Lahaina Fried Soup. The Yamafuji family served this dish, which is a noodle recipe not a soup, for decades at the restaurant and, even now, they make it for fundraisers. A member of the family conjectured it was called that because it was made in the same large pot that the soup was made. A restaurant in Lahaina has Lahaina fried soup on their menu, but the word is out that it is not the same as **Liberty Restaurant's.**

Two Maui girls cruising Lahaina one day remember having a craving for the 'ono rice and gravy that was served at **Liberty Restaurant** for 25 cents. Being broke but persistent, they scrounged under the seats and mats of their car and managed to scrape up enough money for two orders.

Yorihito Uchida ran **Happy Valley Tavern** in the 1970s. Some years after the tavern closed, Mr. Uchida opened **Yori's.** Yori served Hawaiian food, alcohol, and good cheer in his new Happy Valley restaurant. Yori approached every person who came to his establishment and personally took their photo with a Polaroid camera. It would then be placed immediately on the wall. It was no wonder everyone felt welcome there.

Short on money or appetite? **Barefoot Boy** in Kahului and **Dairy Queen** in Wailuku had the answer—a hobo lunch in a cup. The restaurants put rice in the bottom and the customer ordered the top— mahimahi, teri beef, chili, hamburger steak, etc. **Barefoot Boy,** located on Lono Avenue, opened in 1961 and later became **Shirley's. Kapalua Village Store** thinks hobo lunches are such a good idea that they are now offering them on their current menu.

Dairy Queen, Wailuku, fronts its rival, Hokama's TV Service.

Sweet Maui Endings

What could be better on a chilly Maui night than a warm Mango and Kula Strawberry Crisp? (At Kula Country Farms, you can even pick your own strawberries!) Who can resist a Molokai Sweet Potato Pie with a simple pie crust and our favorite sweet potatoes? On Fat Tuesday, why not try some Pumpkin Malasadas from "Vovo," Rick Texeira's grandma?

I did my best to include all my favorite desserts. Using fresh, good quality local fruits will bring out the essence of each dish. I'm sure you'll agree that the melding of Maui flavors in these recipes is just perfect!

Pineapple Pudding Cake

Yield: 8 Servings

3 tablespoons unsalted
   butter
4 large eggs, at room
   temperature
½ + ¼ cup granulated sugar
¼ cup all-purpose flour,
   sifted
¼ teaspoon salt
1 cup buttermilk, at room
   temperature
1 tablespoon fresh lemon
   juice
¼ cup pineapple juice
   (from the Maui Gold
   pineapple; see below)

*For the caramelized
   pineapple:*
1 Maui Gold Pineapple

For the caramel:
2 cups granulated sugar
1 cup water
1 tablespoon lemon juice

For the pineapple sauce:
2 cups granulated sugar
1 cup of water
2 cups finely chopped Maui
   Gold Pineapple
1 tablespoon lemon juice

*T*his scrumptious dessert shows off our wonderful Maui Gold pineapple. The pineapple is caramelized, then chopped up and served in a sauce to go over the pineapple juice-flavored pudding cake.

You'll need three tablespoons of fresh lemon juice for this recipe. You might be able to squeeze out three tablespoons of juice from one big juicy lemon or just use two lemons.

Because the cake should be chilled before serving, make it earlier in the day if you're serving it after dinner.

To make the caramelized pineapple, start by preheating the oven to 350 degrees. Trim and core a Maui Gold Pineapple. Cut it into 1-inch thick slices, lengthwise. Arrange the slices on a baking pan, in one layer, and bake them for 45 minutes. Set the pineapple aside to cool. When it has cooled, pour off the juice. Use this juice in the pudding cake. Finely chop the remaining pineapple meat.

To make the caramel for the bottoms of the ramekins, put the sugar in the saucepan, add the water, and swirl to mix. Bring the syrup to a boil over high heat, stirring or whisking the entire time. Keep it boiling; it will darken as it cooks. When the sugar syrup is a light golden brown, remove it from the heat and stir in the lemon juice. Butter the bottoms of 8 (6 ounce) ramekins and evenly distribute caramel.

To make the pineapple sauce, wash out the saucepan you used to make the caramel and return it to the stove. Add sugar and water again, stir to dissolve, and repeat the caramelizing process. When the caramel is a light golden brown, remove it from the heat and stir in the chopped Maui Gold pineapple and the lemon juice. When the sauce has cooled, store it in a covered container in the refrigerator.

To make the pudding cake, preheat the oven to 350 degrees again. Arrange the ramekins in a large baking pan with high sides.

Melt the butter in the microwave (in short bursts; do not let it burn) or in a small saucepan. Set it aside to cool.

Separate the eggs. You'll need 4 egg whites but only 3 egg yolks, so when you're separating the eggs, put the last egg yolk in a covered container and put it in the refrigerator to use in another dish.

(recipe continued on page 202)

Put the melted butter, ½ cup of the sugar, and the 3 egg yolks in a large bowl and whisk them together until the mixture is smooth and light; this should take about 1 minute.

Sift together the flour and the salt. Add the sifted dry ingredients and the buttermilk to the butter-sugar-egg mixture. Stir until just blended; do not over-mix. Whisk in the lemon and pineapple juices.

Put the egg whites in the bowl of your stand mixer or in a large bowl. Beat the egg whites until they can hold a soft peak. Reduce the speed of the mixer (if using a mixer) and sprinkle the remaining ¼ cup of sugar over the egg whites. Beat the egg whites at high speed until the whites can hold a firm but not stiff peak.

Spoon ⅓ of the beaten egg whites onto the egg yolk mixture and gently fold to blend. Fold the remaining whites into the batter.

Spoon the mixture into the ramekins. Divide the batter evenly. The ramekins should be filled to the top. Put the baking pan in the preheated oven and pour just enough hot water into the pan to reach half-way up the ramekins. (If you put the water in the pan and then try to move the pan in the oven, the water is going to slosh out of the pan.)

Bake the cakes until the tops are puffed and golden. This should take about 25 to 30 minutes. Remove from oven and chill for 2 to 24 hours before serving.

PRESENTATION

Set out 8 dessert plates. Invert a ramekin of cake over each plate and gently ease the caramel-topped cake onto the platter. Spoon pineapple caramel sauce over the cakes and serve.

Portuguese Sweet Bread Pudding

Bread pudding gets a local twist when you use Portuguese sweet bread and Big Island vanilla beans or vanilla extract. For extra deliciousness, you can make this pudding with Portuguese sweet bread that you've baked yourself; see the recipe on page 8.

Yield: 1 (8 x 8-inch) Loaf

6 cups cubed Portuguese bread (1-inch cubes, lightly toasted; see instructions in recipe)
2 cups whole milk
9 large eggs
1 vanilla bean
   OR 2 teaspoons vanilla extract
1 cup sugar
2 tablespoons cinnamon
2 teaspoons ground ginger
1 teaspoon nutmeg
½ teaspoon salt
1 cup white chocolate chips

Preheat oven to 350 degrees; butter a 13 x 9-inch baking dish.

Cut the Portuguese sweet bread into 1-inch cubes. Spread the cubes over 2 baking sheets (in single layers; don't heap up the cubes) and toast in the 350-degree oven for approximately 20 minutes, or until crisp and slightly browned. Check on them occasionally—don't let them burn!

If using the vanilla bean, cut it open lengthwise and scrape out the seeds in the center. Put the scrapings into the milk. The pods will still have some flavor, so save them to use in another recipe. Try adding them to a covered container of sugar and letting the mixture sit for a few days; you'll have vanilla sugar.

If using vanilla extract, add the extract to the milk. Add the sugar, cinnamon, ginger, nutmeg, and salt. Mix well and put over medium heat. Bring the milk mixture to a boil; remove the pan from the heat immediately. Do not let the milk boil for more than a few seconds.

Add about ¼ cup of the hot milk to the beaten eggs, whisking as you add. Add another ¼ cup or so, continuing to whisk. Keep adding milk until the eggs are close to the temperature of the milk still left in the pan. You can then pour the egg and milk mixture into the saucepan and whisk to combine.

Add the white chocolate pieces to the saucepan and mix well.

Put the toasted bread cubes in the buttered baking dish. Spread them in an even layer. Slowly pour the milk custard over the bread. Make sure that all of the bread has been coated with custard.

You can slide the pan into the oven at this point, if you must. However, the pudding will be creamier if you let the pan sit on the counter for ½ hour or so, to soften the bread.

Bake the pudding in the center of the preheated oven for about 1 hour, or until a small knife inserted in the center of the pudding comes out clean.

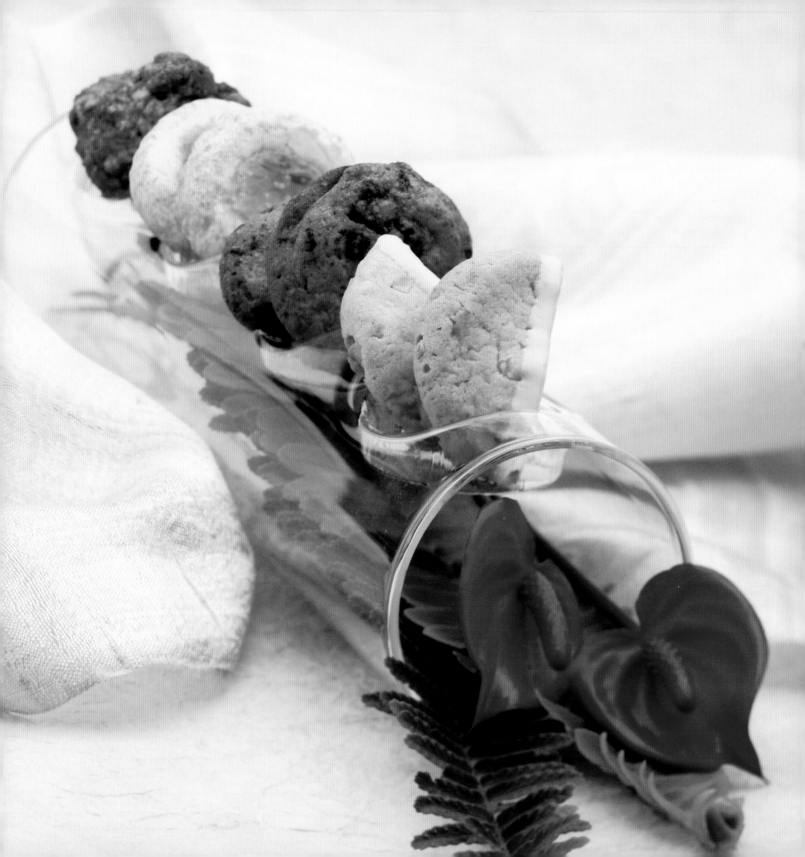

Pohā Berry Ginger Thumbprint Cookies

Edible ginger does not come from the same plant as the ginger flower. It was brought to Hawai'i by Asian immigrants and has become a staple Island spice added to many dishes for distinct flavoring.

Yield: 18 cookies

2 cups all-purpose flour
½ teaspoon baking powder
½ teaspoon salt
¾ cup unsalted butter, softened
⅔ cup sugar
3 teaspoons peeled and grated ginger
1 large egg
½ cup Maui raw sugar (to roll on outside of cookies)
¼ cup pohā berry jam

Preheat the oven to 350 degrees. Cover a cookie sheet with parchment paper and lightly grease or butter the paper.

Sift the flour, baking powder, and salt together into a bowl. Cream the butter and sugar. Peel and grate the ginger. Add the ginger and the egg to the butter and sugar and mix until just combined. Add ½ of the dry ingredients, mix, and add the other half. Do not over-mix.

Form the dough into 1-inch balls. You can do this with a cookie or ice cream scoop, or you can roll the dough into a long roll and break off chunks of the roll to form into balls.

Roll the balls in a bowl of Maui raw sugar. Place the cookies about 2 inches apart on the prepared baking sheet. Press a thumbprint into the center of each ball; the print should be about ½-inch deep. Fill each print with about ¾ teaspoon of jam.

Bake the cookies until the edges are golden, about 15 minutes in the 350 degree oven.

Macadamia Nut Cookies

Yield: 24 (3-inch) cookies

1 stick butter
¾ cup granulated sugar
1 large egg
1⅓ cups cake flour
1 teaspoon baking powder
¼ teaspoon salt
½ cup chopped macadamia nuts

Cream the butter and sugar. Add the beaten egg and mix well. Sift together the flour, baking powder, and salt. Add the dry ingredients to the butter and egg mixture in three parts, beating after each addition. Fold in the chopped macadamia nuts.

Use a 1-ounce scoop to make balls of cookie dough. Space the balls evenly on an ungreased cookie sheet. Bake the cookies at 325 degrees for 15 to 20 minutes.

Chocolate Chunk Cookies

Yield: 24 (3-inch) cookies

½ cup (1 stick) butter
½ cup granulated sugar
½ cup brown sugar
1 egg, beaten
1¼ cup all-purpose flour
1 teaspoon baking soda
1 teaspoon salt
1 cup chocolate chips

This classic chocolate cookie is a favorite. Use moist dark brown sugar rather than hardened, which will dry the cookies. Choose the best chocolate chip you can buy.

Preheat oven to 325 degrees.

Cream the butter and sugar. Add the beaten eggs and mix well. Sift together the flour, baking soda, and salt. Add the dry ingredients to the butter and egg mixture in three parts, beating after each addition. Fold in the chocolate chips.

Use a 1-ounce scoop to make balls of cookie dough. Space the balls evenly on an ungreased cookie sheet. Bake the cookies at 325 degrees for 15 to 20 minutes.

Tropical Oatmeal Cookies

Yield: 18 (3-inch) cookies

1 cup butter, salted, at
   room temperature
⅓ cup white sugar
1 cup brown sugar, packed
4 eggs
½ teaspoon vanilla extract
1⅜ cup all-purpose flour
½ teaspoon salt
1 tablespoon baking soda
1 tablespoon cinnamon
¼ teaspoon nutmeg
3 cups oats, old-fashioned
1 cup walnut pieces
½ cup raisins
½ cup dried pineapple,
   chopped

Preheat the oven to 325 degrees.

Line baking pans with parchment paper.

Cream the butter and the white and brown sugar together, mix 5 minutes on medium speed or by hand.

Beat the eggs. Add the eggs and vanilla to the butter and sugar. Mix well.

Sift together the flour, salt, baking soda, cinnamon, and nutmeg. Add the dry ingredients to the dough and mix again.

If you're starting with whole walnuts, and dried pineapple, chop them coarsely. Add the walnuts, pineapple, and raisins to the dough and mix. You may want to fold them into the dough with a spatula.

With a spoon or a scoop, make 1-inch balls of cookie dough. Arrange on the prepared baking sheet, 1-inch apart, and bake for approximately 25 minutes. If your oven bakes unevenly, you may want to take the sheet out after 15 minutes and turn it around before putting it back in the oven.

Take the cookies from the oven when they are a golden brown. Remove the cookies from the sheet immediately and cool on wire racks.

Dried mango slices, coconut flakes, currants, or any dried mixed fruits may be substituted for the raisins.

Sake Lychee Kanten

*K*anten is the Japanese name for agar-agar, a gelatinous thickening agent often used to make Asian desserts. It is processed from seaweed, and comes in either powder, flake, or strip form. Here, kanten thickens the sake and lychee juice: an odd, implausible pairing that will surprise and delight you.

Mix the sake and lychee juice in a small saucepan. Add the kanten; let it soak for 30 minutes. Set the saucepan over medium heat and bring the mixture to a boil. Boil until the kanten has completely dissolved.

Pour the mixture into molds or a 9 x 13-inch pan. Add the raspberries to the molds or pan, distributing them as evenly as you can. Let the jelly cool in the refrigerator.

PRESENTATION

If you've made this jelly in the 9 x 13-inch pan, cut it into bite-sized pieces. If you've made it in molds, unmold it. Serve after a meal as a light and palate-refreshing dessert.

What you don't eat immediately can be stored in the refrigerator.

Yield: 1 (9 x 13 inch) pan

1 cup Saki Snow sake
   OR your favorite sake
1 cup lychee purée or juice
½ cup sugar
¾ strip kanten (agar-agar)
   (about ⅛ ounce of
   kanten)
2 cups fresh raspberries

Coconut Custard Pie

*Y*ou can make your own pie shell or take a shortcut with a purchased one from the supermarket. The coconut flakes will rise to the top, creating a coarse texture on the top surface. Coconut lovers, enjoy!

Preheat oven to 300 degrees.

Beat the eggs lightly; add the rest of the ingredients and mix well.

Pour into the pie shell and bake at 300 degrees for about 1 hour.

Cool before serving.

Yield: 1 (9-inch) pie

1 (9-inch) unbaked pie shell

For the filling:
2 cups eggs (about 8 large
   eggs, beaten)
1 cup sugar
½ teaspoon salt
½ tablespoon vanilla
4 cups milk
1 teaspoon nutmeg
1½ cups coconut flakes

Moloka'i Sweet Potato Pie

Yield: 2 (9-inch) pies

2 (9-inch) pie shells, unbaked

½ cup (1 stick) butter, softened

2 cups cooked and mashed Moloka'i sweet potatoes

2 cups granulated sugar

½ cup + 2 tablespoons evaporated milk; this would be 1 (5-ounce) can

1 teaspoon vanilla extract

3 eggs, beaten

1½ teaspoons cinnamon

Our own Moloka'i purple sweet potatoes star in this easy pie, which appears in recipes from chefs Emeril Lagasse, Sam Choy and Perry Bateman. Other good varieties are the Molokai Gold and the universal orange variety. The sweet potato is an excellent source of vitamin A. It became an overnight crop during World War II, when Hawai'i experienced shortages of imported food. It has a long history in the Islands. The early Hawaiians called the tuber 'uala' and either baked it in the imu or grated it raw for a pudding mixed with coconut milk and then wrapped in ti leaves to bake in the imu.

Preheat the oven to 350 degrees.

Put the butter, potatoes, sugar, and evaporated milk into a large bowl and mix well. Add the vanilla, eggs, and cinnamon and mix again. Pour into the prepared pie shells. Bake in the 350-degree oven for about 1 hour, or until set. Cool and serve.

Chocolate Fondue with Seasonal Fruit

Fondue was the last word in sophistication in the 1960s and then fell out of favor. Now it's trendy again, and for many of the same reasons that it was once popular. It tastes great, it isn't difficult to make or present, and guests have a lot of fun dipping their own dessert.

You're not limited to dipping fruit. This fondue is also great with chunks of pound cake, cheesecake, coconut macaroons, marshmallows, or even Rice Krispies treats. Be creative and have fun!

If there's any leftover chocolate sauce, store it in the refrigerator. You can reheat it for another round of fondue, OR, you can spread it between two pieces of bread, dip the bread in beaten egg, and make chocolate French toast.

Prepare the banana, strawberries, kiwi, and pineapple per the instructions in the ingredients list. Arrange on a serving platter.

Pour the heavy cream, evaporated milk, and corn syrup into a small saucepan. Place on the stove and bring the mixture to a boil over medium heat. Transfer the hot mixture to a mixing bowl. Add the chocolate and mix until the chocolate has melted and you have a smooth fondue sauce.

PRESENTATION

If you have a fondue set, pour the chocolate sauce into the fondue pot and turn on the heat. This may mean flicking a switch or turning a dial, if you have an electric fondue set, or it may mean lighting a can of Sterno or a candle. If you don't have a fondue set, you can use a butter warmer with a tea light, or perhaps just a saucepan on a hot-plate.

Set out the platter of fresh fruit or other goodies, a stack of dessert plates, and an array of skewers. Guests skewer their choice of fruit or goodie, dip it in the chocolate, and enjoy!

Yield: 3 servings

1 banana, peeled, cut in 1½-inch thick slices
6 strawberries, with stem on, for dipping
1 kiwi, peeled, cut in 6 wedges
¼ pineapple, peeled and cored, diced into 1-inch cubes
½ cup heavy cream
¼ cup evaporated milk
1 tablespoon corn syrup
½ pound chocolate chunks or chips

Cascarones

*P*hillip Quiocho, one of our bakers, shares this family recipe with us. These unusual cascarones are flavored with ground lavender. You can buy culinary lavender from Maui's own Ali'i Kula Lavender, or you can use any culinary lavender. The lavender will come as dried flowers. To make ground lavender, pulverize the flowers with a spice grinder or a mortar and pestle.

Mix all ingredients for the cascarones; they will make a stiff dough. Roll the dough into 1-inch diameter balls.

Heat the oil in your deep-fryer or a deep pot to 325 degrees. Slip a few balls of dough into the oil and fry, turning as needed, until they are golden brown. Drain on paper towels. Repeat until all the cascarones have been fried.

To make the glaze, add the brown sugar and water to a deep pot over medium heat. Bring the mixture to a boil and cook until the sugar syrup reaches the soft ball stage. If some of the syrup is dropped into cold water, it will form a soft ball. You can test the syrup with a candy thermometer; the syrup should read 234 to 240 degrees. Remove from the heat and stir in the butter.

Pour the glaze over the cascarones.

Yield: 1 dozen cascarones

1 (16-ounce) box mochiko flour
1 tablespoon ground lavender
1 egg, beaten
½ cup coconut milk
½ cup evaporated milk
Oil for deep-frying

For the glaze:
1 cup brown sugar
2 tablespoons water
2 tablespoons butter

Pumpkin Malasadas

Yield: 2 dozen malasadas

1½ tablespoons
   (2 packages) yeast
1 cup warm water
⅓ cup butter, melted
6 eggs, beaten
1 cup evaporated milk
½ cup sugar
1 teaspoon salt
7 cups all-purpose flour
   (no need sift)
1 (15-ounce) can pumpkin
   purée
Oil for deep-frying
½ cup sugar, for sprinkling

This is a generation's-old recipe that was originally from Grandma. Now, Marlene Texeira, makes the Fat Tuesday malasadas every year. She wakes up before dawn to mix the dough, and because Kula is so cold, she has to put an electric blanket over the bowl so the dough will rise.

She used to use a big soup pot to heat the oil, but now she uses a wok.

If you're feeling energetic, you can harvest a few of the sweet pumpkins from your garden, cook them, purée them, and use the purée in these tasty malasadas. If you're harried and hurried, use canned purée.

Mix the yeast and warm water in a small bowl and let it sit while you mix the other liquids. This gives the yeast a head start, away from the salt, which retards its growth.

Melt the butter in a small saucepan or in the microwave (in short bursts, watching it so that it doesn't burn). Beat the eggs in a large bowl. (You may not be able to use your stand mixer for this, unless it can handle extra-large batches of dough.) Add the evaporated milk, sugar, and salt. Mix in the butter, which should have cooled down. Finally, add the dissolved yeast.

Add a cup or two of the flour to the butter and egg mixture and mix. Add some of the pumpkin purée and mix. Alternate adding flour and purée until all of the flour and the purée have been added to the dough.

Cover the bowl and put it in a warm spot to rise. Let it rise for about 1 hour, or until the dough has doubled in size.

Heat the oil in your deep-fryer or a large pot to 350 degrees. Add a few scoops of dough to the oil. Some people use a tablespoon; some people use a kitchen spoon; some people use a small ice cream scoop; some people use their hands. How you scoop is up to you. Fry the malasadas until they're golden brown all over, turning them as necessary. You will definitely have to do this in several batches. Do not crowd the oil.

Drain the cooked malasadas on paper towels. Roll in a pan of granulated sugar, or shake in a bag full of sugar.

Best served warm.

Pumpkin Pie, Kula-Style

Yield: 1 (8-inch) pie

Pie Crust (8-inch pie pan):
1 cup all-purpose flour
½ teaspoon salt
½ cup Butter Crisco
¼ cup water

Pumpkin Filling:
1 fresh pumpkin (about
    2 pounds, should make
    2 cups)
2 eggs
½ cup white sugar
¼ cup brown sugar
½ teaspoon salt
1 teaspoon ground
    cinnamon
½ teaspoon ground ginger
    OR you may use 1½
    teaspoon pumpkin pie
    spice in place of the
    cinnamon and ginger
¼ teaspoon ground cloves
¾ can (9 fl. ounces) of a 12
    fl. ounce can evaporated
    milk

*A*unty Judy shares this recipe using fresh sweet pumpkins from her Kula garden.

She has baked pumpkin pies in large batches (sometimes 15 or 20) for various fundraisers and to give away at Thanksgiving. Each pie is made with lots of TLC, and those who are fortunate enough to receive one feel truly grateful.

Judy's daughter, Jody, was always in charge of the crust. "I can't count how many pie crusts I have made," she laughs.

Use fresh pumpkin if you can, because it has a richer flavor.

PIE CRUST

Preheat oven to 350 degrees.

Mix flour, salt, and cut in Butter Crisco with a pastry blender or 2 knives; slowly add water (while mixing) until everything comes together in a ball. Roll out the dough, approximately ⅛-inch thickness, and place into an 8-inch pie pan. Pat into place and crimp the edges. Set aside until pie filling is ready.

PUMPKIN FILLING

Peel the pumpkin, remove the seeds, slice the pumpkin. Place in a pot with water until slices are covered. Cook until soft. Drain the liquid, place the pumpkin in a blender, and mix until smooth.

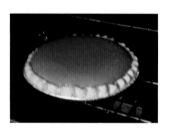

Add all dry ingredients, eggs, and milk to the blender with the puréed pumpkin. Mix until smooth. Pour into pie crust and bake at 350 degrees for 50 to 55 minutes. Insert a toothpick into the center of the pie, if it comes out clean, it's done.

Cool and serve with your favorite whipped cream or ice cream.

Pumpkin Ladies

Judy Silva and Marlene Texeira are known to their family as the pumpkin ladies. From the pumpkins they grow in their yard, they make malasadas, pies, and all kinds of other tasty desserts. And they don't just grow pumpkins but other fruits and vegetables, too: lettuce, onions, tomatoes, peaches, plums—many of which they pickle and give away to friends and relatives.

When asked what kinds of pumpkins they grow, Judy and Marlene say they don't know. The old pumpkins that were left in the patch just germinated and sprouted! Their garden is so fertile (or maybe it's the pumpkin ladies' magic touch) that everything just pops up out of the ground, sweet, plump, and delicious. And it's not just their garden that's bountiful; it's all of Kula. The plum trees and hydrangea plants Judy and Marlene's grandfather planted at Polipoli State Park when he was a ranger there have now spread over the area and are still thriving, over a hundred years later.

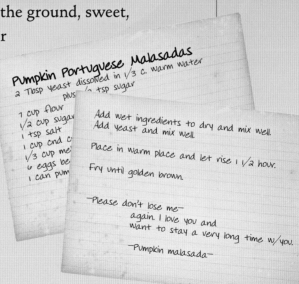

Pumpkin Portuguese Malasadas
2 Tbsp yeast dissolved in 1/3 c. warm water
plus 1/2 tsp sugar

7 cup flour
1/2 cup sugar
1 tsp salt
1 cup cnd c...
1/3 cup me...
6 eggs be...
1 can pum...

Add wet ingredients to dry and mix well.
Add yeast and mix well.

Place in warm place and let rise 1 1/2 hour.

Fry until golden brown.

—Please don't lose me—
again. I love you and
want to stay a very long time w/you.

—Pumpkin malasada—

Almond Float

A lmond float is a simplified recipe made with almond extract. The traditional Chinese almond curd is made with ground almonds and is best served with canned fruit cocktail. But first try this dish with fresh fruit rather than canned. Strawberries, raspberries, kiwi, mandarin oranges, and lychee are good choices.

Soak agar-agar for 30 minutes in the 7 cups of water, then boil until mostly dissolved. Strain the agar-agar water through a sieve, to remove any lumps, and mix with the sugar, evaporated milk, and almond extract. Pour the mixture equally into two 9 x 13-inch glass baking dishes.

Agar-agar will jell at room temperature, but you will probably want to put the mixture into the refrigerator, so that the float will be nicely chilled. Cut into ½-inch squares or diamonds and serve with the cut-up fresh fruit.

Yield: 1 (9 x 13-inch) pan

4 sticks kanten (agar-agar)
7 cups water
2¾ cups sugar
4 cups evaporated milk
5 teaspoons almond extract
6 cups assorted peeled and
  cut fresh fruit

Mango and Kula Strawberry Crisp

Yield: 8 servings

3 cups ripe mangoes,
   peeled and thinly sliced
2 cups Kula strawberries,
   stems removed, cut in
   half
1 + ½ teaspoon ground
   cinnamon
¼ teaspoon nutmeg
1 tablespoon lemon juice
¼ cup butter (softened)
½ cup brown sugar
   (packed)
½ cup flour

*T*he "king of fruits," arrived in Hawai'i in the early 1800s and is still popular as a backyard tree.

The success of this recipe depends on the quality of the mangoes. (Everyone on Maui knows the best mangoes are from the Yee's Orchard in Kīhei.) Piries, Haydens, Gouveias, Ma'apulehu, and numerous other varieties can all be found in Kā'anapali and are all 'ono.

Celebrate mango season with this luscious crisp. Kula strawberries, grown in Haleakalā's rich volcanic soil, are the perfect complement to sweet Maui mangoes.

Prepare the mangoes and strawberries according to the instructions in the ingredients list. Butter a 9 x 9-inch glass baking dish. Preheat the oven to 350 degrees.

Mix the sliced mangoes and strawberries with 1 teaspoon of the cinnamon, the nutmeg, and the lemon juice. Put the mixture in the buttered glass baking dish.

Blend the butter and brown sugar. Cut in the flour and the remaining ½ teaspoon cinnamon with a pastry cutter or your hands until you have a mixture like coarse cornmeal.

Sprinkle the topping evenly over the mangoes and strawberries.

Bake for 15 to 20 minutes; the topping should be golden brown.

PRESENTATION

This crisp is best when served warm. Add a spoonful of vanilla ice cream or a dash of cream if desired.

Shave Ice

Shave ice can be considered Hawai'i's official state treat. It's found everywhere—mom and pop stores, malls, lunchwagons, fairs, festivals. Unlike the mainland snow cone made with ground ice, Hawai'i uses fine shaved ice so all the flavorings dissolve into the ice. It came to the islands via Japanese immigrants who, after they left the plantations to start family-run grocery stores, featured shave ice as a specialty. In this recipe, instead of flavored syrups, we add fresh fruits. You don't need an expensive electric shave ice machine to enjoy this cool and refreshing treat. There are hand-cranked shave ice machines that come with the molds to freeze the ice for shaving.

Yield: 2 servings

4 cups freshly shaved ice
6 tablespoons sweetened red bean paste (koshian)
4 strawberries, trimmed, cut in half
1 kiwi, peeled and cut into 6 wedges
1 orange, peeled and cut into segments
2 each mochi filled with vanilla ice cream
½ cup sweetened condensed milk

Shave ice into two serving bowls. Top ice with the azuki beans, vanilla mochi ice cream, and fresh fruit arranged nicely. Pour sweetened condensed milk over and serve.

Liliko'i Crème Brûlée

Yield: 6 servings

1 cup heavy cream
1 cup milk
½ cup sugar
½ cup pasteurized egg
  yolks
1 teaspoon vanilla extract
¼ cup liliko'i juice
  (concentrated)
2 tablespoons sugar
2 tablespoons brown sugar

*B*oth liliko'i and passion fruit are known as water lemons. Passion fruit is the sour yellow variety while the purple-skinned liliko'i is sweeter, growing wild in the mountains where its prolific vine bears fruit during summer and fall. Years ago, a liliko'i would be used as a children's pacifier. Smaller than a lemon, it has a rich aroma and flavor.

In a saucepan bring ½ of the milk and cream mixture to a boil. Take the remaining milk and cream and beat in the egg yolks, then slowly temper all of the hot cream with the cold cream/yolk mixture.

Add vanilla and liliko'i juice at this stage. Pour into 6 small ramekins.

Then bake in a water bath for approx 35 to 40 minutes or until it stops moving.

Remove from oven and cool to room temperature.

Refrigerate for 1 hour, or overnight.

Heat the broiler to high. Mix the 2 tablespoons of sugar and the brown sugar in a small bowl. Sprinkle evenly over the top of the custard. Place the custard about 2 inches from the broiler and broil until the sugar melts; this should take about 2 minutes. Watch the custard carefully, as it will go from melting to burning very quickly.

A home torch would also work.

Remove from heat and allow to cool. Serve.

Pineapple-Carrot Cake

Yield: 2 (9-inch) cakes

2 cups finely shredded,
  organic carrots
1 cup Maui Gold pineapple,
  small diced
3 cups all-purpose flour
1 tablespoon cinnamon
1½ teaspoons baking soda
½ teaspoon salt
4 large eggs
1½ cups organic canola oil
2½ cups sugar

Carrot cake gets even better when it's made with fresh local produce. We like to use Hāna organic red carrots and Maui Gold pineapple, a sweet, low-acid pineapple that works beautifully in baked goods. If you can't get the Hāna carrots, use the sweetest, tastiest organic carrots that you can find. It makes a big difference in the flavor.

Peel and finely shred the carrots. Peel and core the pineapple, if starting with a whole pineapple, and cut the meat into ¼-inch chunks.

Preheat oven to 350 degrees. Oil and flour two 9-inch cake pans.

Sift together the flour, cinnamon, baking soda, and salt. Beat the 4 eggs; mix the eggs, sugar, and oil. Add about ⅓ of the dry ingredients to the egg-oil mixture and mix well. Repeat until all the dry ingredients have been added. Fold in the grated carrots and cut-up pineapple.

Pour the batter into the oiled and floured pans. Bake in the 350-degree oven for about 35 to 40 minutes, or until a toothpick or paring knife inserted in the middle of the cake comes out clean.

Remove the cakes from the pans and cool on a wire rack. You can serve the sliced cake dusted with powdered sugar and freshly whipped cream.

Banana Lumpia

(Courtesy of Amber Fontanilla)

Yield: 8 lumpia

4 apple bananas (Maui-grown if possible), cut in half lengthwise
1 cup brown sugar
1 tablespoon ground cinnamon
1 egg, beaten
8 lumpia wrappers
2 cups vegetable oil, for frying

Banana lumpia can be frozen after they're rolled up in their wrappers. Defrost them completely before frying.

If your family loves these lumpia, make and freeze a double or triple batch. If you can assemble the gang around the kitchen table to help you prepare the bananas and roll up the lumpia, you'll finish in no time.

Mix the brown sugar and cinnamon in a shallow pan. Peel and cut up the bananas.

Roll the sliced bananas in brown sugar and cinnamon until they are completely coated. Lay them out on a plate or a piece of wax paper. Beat the egg in a small bowl.

Lay one wrapper on the table or counter in front of you, one of the pointed ends pointing at you. Lay one of the coated banana halves across the wrapper, parallel to the edge of the table. Fold the bottom of the wrapper up over the banana. Fold the right and left edges of the wrapper inward. The wrapper should now look like an envelope, flap open. Start rolling up the lumpia. When there's only a triangle of wrapper left, brush some egg on the inside of the wrapper and push it against the lumpia. The egg will dry and seal the lumpia shut.

Repeat until all the lumpia are rolled.

Bring the frying oil to 350 degrees, either in your deep-fryer or in a deep pot. Add the lumpia, a few at a time, and fry them until they are golden brown on all sides. Remove and drain on paper towels.

Green Tea Shortbread Cookies

Shortbread gets a local twist when it's made with matcha (Japanese green tea powder), and sprinkled with Maui mango sugar or crunchy Maui raw sugar.

Preheat the oven to 350 degrees. Put a layer of parchment paper over a cookie sheet.

Sift together the flour and the salt.

Beat the butter and sugar until creamy. (A stand mixer is best for this.) Add the matcha, little by little, mixing as you add. When the mixture is evenly green, scrape down the sides of the mixing bowl and mix for another 3 minutes, or until the butter-sugar mixture is light and fluffy.

Add the sifted dry ingredients in installments, mixing on low speed. The finished dough will be crumbly rather than soft and wet.

Roll out the dough on a lightly floured pastry board or mat, or just a counter or table. It should be ½-inch thick. You may need to put a sheet of wax paper on top to keep the dough from crumbling as you roll it. Use cookie cutters to cut out cookies. Re-roll the leftover dough and cut out more cookies.

Carefully transfer the cookies to the parchment-covered cookie sheet. Sprinkle the Maui mango sugar over the top of the cookies. Bake in the preheated oven for approximately 15 minutes. The edges should be lightly browned. Cool on wire racks before serving.

Yield: 1 dozen cookies

2¼ cups all-purpose flour
¼ teaspoon salt
1 cup (2 sticks) unsalted butter
1 to 2 tablespoons matcha (green tea powder)
½ cup sugar
1 teaspoon Maui mango sugar, for topping OR substitute Maui raw sugar

Glossary

A

Achiote Seeds: Seeds from the lipstick plant, also called annatto or achuete.

'Ahi: Hawaiian name for yellowfin or bigeye tuna. Served in the Islands as sashimi. Substitute fresh blackfin or bluefin tuna.

Aioli: Garlic mayonnaise.

Aku: The Hawaiian name for skipjack tuna. Deep red in color and stronger tasting than 'ahi. Good broiled, grilled, or used raw in poke. Substitute any tuna.

'Alaea salt: Hawaiian name for a red-tinged sea salt. Iron-rich "red dirt" gives it its color. Substitute sea salt.

B

Banana leaves: Used to wrap food cooked in an earth oven (see IMU). Substitute aluminum foil or parchment paper, corn husks, or TI LEAVES.

Bean sprouts: Sprouted mung beans. Consumed raw or lightly stir-fried. Substitute canned mung beans.

Bean thread noodles: Thin, transparent noodles made from ground mung beans.

Black beans: Substitute other firm beans.

Bok choy: A type of cabbage used in Chinese cuisine.

Breadfruit: A bland, starchy vegetable used in the Pacific Islands. Substitute potatoes.

C

Calamari: Another name for SQUID. Substitute octopus.

Capers: Substitute chopped green olives.

Char siu: Chinese sweet roasted pork.

Chinese five-spice powder: A fragrant, spicy, and slightly sweet spice mixture made from ground star anise, Szechuan peppercorns, fennel seeds, cloves, and cinnamon.

Cilantro: Also called Chinese parsley. The green leaves and stems of the CORIANDER plant. Substitute parsley.

Coconut milk: The rich, creamy liquid extracted by squeezing the grated meat of a coconut. Available fresh, canned, or frozen. Substitute (thin) use: 1 cup whole milk beaten with 1 teaspoon coconut flavoring; (thick) use: 1 cup heavy cream with 1 teaspoon coconut flavoring.

Coriander seeds: Seeds of the coriander plant. Closely related to caraway, fennel, dill, and anise.

Cumin: The seeds of a flowering plant native to the Mediterranean and Asia. Used as whole seed or as powder.

Curry powder: A mixture of spices including cardamom, chili, cinnamon, cloves, CORIANDER, CUMIN, fennel seeds, fenugreek, mace, nutmeg, red and black pepper, saffron, SESAME SEEDS, tamarind, and turmeric. Different curry powders use different spices in different proportions.

D

Daikon: A large Asian radish, usually white in color used in Japan and Korea for soups and pickles, or eaten raw. Flavors range from mild to spicy-hot. Available fresh, pickled, or preserved. Substitute turnips or radish.

Daikon sprouts: See KAIWARE.

Dashi: A clear, light Japanese fish broth sold as instant stock in granules or tea-like bags, or as a concentrate. Substitute chicken stock.

Dill: An aromatic herb with needle-like leaves, small yellow flowers, and pungent flavor. Used fresh or dried.

F

Fish sauce: A concentrated salty brown liquid typically made from anchovies fermented in brine. Used in Southeast Asian cooking. Substitute 1 part SHOYU plus 4 parts mashed anchovies.

Furikake: A Japanese condiment made from dried seaweed flakes, SESAME SEEDS, bonito flakes, sugar, salt, and other seasonings. Substitute ground sesame seeds and finely chopped NORI seaweed sheets.

G

Ginger: The root of the domestic ginger plant. It is used as a seasoning both in savory dishes and in sweets. (Powdered ginger is not a good substitute.)

Gochujang: Korean chili paste. May also contain BLACK BEANS, garlic, and spices. Also spelled kochujang. Substitute any chili paste.

Guava

Guava: A round tropical fruit with a yellow skin and pink inner flesh and many seeds. Grown commercially in Hawai'i. The purée or juice is available as a frozen concentrate. Substitute LILIKO'I.

H

Hagi: Japanese word for triggerfish, the brightly colored reef fishes. Many genera and species of triggerfishes.

Hawaiian chili pepper: A small, hot chili pepper grown in Hawai'i. Substitute Thai bird chilies or any small hot chili pepper.

Hawaiian chili-pepper water: Water infused with chopped HAWAIIAN CHILI PEPPERS (sometimes garlic is added). It is very popular locally. Substitute water infused with any hot chili pepper.

Hawaiian salt: Coarse, heavy, white or red crystals made from evaporated seawater. Substitute kosher salt or sea salt.

He'e: Hawaiian word for octopus. See TAKO.

Hibachi: A small, portable, inexpensive Japanese outdoor grill.

Hoisin sauce: A thick reddish-brown sauce made with fermented soybeans, garlic, rice, salt, and sugar. Substitute pureed plum baby food mixed with SHOYU, garlic, and chili peppers.

Hondashi: Japanese fish broth powder.

I

Imu: The old Hawai'i underground earth oven lined with fire-heated stones covered with banana stalks and BANANA LEAVES.

'Inamona: Hawaiian word for a relish (in paste or chopped form) made from roasted KUKUI NUTS and salt. Substitute coarsely chopped salted cashew nuts.

J

Japanese vinegar: Rice vinegar, milder than white vinegar.

K

Kaffir lime leaves: Glossy, dark-green leaves that have a floral-citrus aroma. Substitute LEMONGRASS or lime zest.

Kaiware: Japanese name for DAIKON radish sprouts. Substitute clover sprouts.

Kalbi: Korean barbecued short ribs.

Kālua: Usually refers to a whole pig cooked in an IMU. Substitute turkey.

Kamaboko: A Japanese seafood product used mostly in Japanese soup or noodle dishes; also called fish cake.

Kiawe: Locally found tree whose wood charcoal (mesquite) is excellent for grilling.

Kim chee: A Korean pickled vegetable usually made with Chinese cabbage (WON BOK), vinegar, salt, garlic, and chili peppers. Can be very hot and spicy. Substitute pickled cucumbers or cabbage with garlic and chili peppers.

Kombu: Dried kelp.

Kukui nuts: Hawaiian name for the candlenut. See also 'INAMONA, a relish made with roasted kukui nuts. Substitute roasted cashew nuts.

L

Laulau: Packages of TI LEAVES or BANANA LEAVES containing pork, beef, salted fish, or TARO tops. Laulau are baked in an IMU or in a regular gas or electric oven.

Lemongrass: A citrus-scented grass with a distinctive lemon flavor and aroma. Its long, woody stalk resembles the white part of a green onion. Substitute lemon zest.

Liliko'i: A tangy, plum-sized, multi-seeded tropical fruit. Also known as passion fruit. Sold as frozen concentrate. Substitute frozen concentrate liliko'i or orange juice.

Limu: Hawaiian word for all types of plants living in the water or damp places. The word now refers to edible seaweeds. Substitute seaweeds with similar characteristics like kelp, KOMBU.

Limu kohu: An edible red seaweed that may range in color from tan through shades of pink to dark red. Hawaiians considered it a great treat. It is generally rolled into balls and dried after it is collected. Substitute kelp.

Limu līpoa: An edible brown seaweed, generally used in a preserved salted form. Substitute kelp.

Long rice: Translucent thread-like noodles made from mung bean flour. Typically needs to be soaked in water before cooking.

Lū'au leaves: The young green tops of the TARO root. Substitute fresh spinach.

Lumpia (wrappers): A thin wheat wrapper filled with minced vegetables, bits of meat, seafood, or TOFU. Served either uncooked or deep-fried.

Lup cheong: Sweet, oily Chinese dried sausage. Substitute PORTUGUESE SAUSAGE.

Lychee: Small round fruit with sweet white flesh.

M

Macadamia nuts: Round, oily nuts with a creamy, slightly crunchy texture, harvested from trees, and grown on the Big Island. Substitute pine nuts.

Mahimahi: Also called dolphinfish, it has a firm, pink flesh. Best fresh but often available frozen. Substitute snapper, catfish, or halibut.

Mango: An oval tropical fruit with golden-orange flesh and an enticing, aromatic flavor; skin color ranges from yellow-orange to burgundy to green. Substitute peaches or sweet ripe nectarines.

Marunggay leaves: Leaves with a citrus-like and slightly bitter flavor, used in Filipino cuisine.

Maui onion: A sweet, mild onion, originally grown in the Kula district of Maui.

Mirin: Japanese sweet rice wine. Substitute cream sherry or sweet vermouth.

Miso: A soybean paste made by salting and fermenting soybeans and rice. Shiro miso, or white miso, is the mildest of several types. Available shrink-wrapped, or in cans and jars. Can be refrigerated for months. Substitute condensed chicken broth blended with a small amount of TOFU.

Mochi: Steamed or pounded rice cake.

Mochiko: Japanese glutinous rice flour used in making pastries and some sauces.

Moi: Hawaiian name for small threadfin fish.

MSG: Monosodium glutamate.

Mushrooms: Most commonly seen mushrooms in Hawai'i are button mushrooms, enoki, oyster mushrooms, portobello mushrooms, and SHIITAKE MUSHROOMS.

Mussels: Bivalve mollusks. Substitute frozen, previously frozen, or canned.

N

Namasu: Japanese salad made with pickled carrots, DAIKON, and vinegar marinade.

Nori: Paper-thin sheets of seasoned, dried seaweed used for SUSHI.

O

Octopus: See TAKO.

Ogo: Japanese name for *Gracilaria* seaweed. Several Hawai'i aquaculture operations grow ogo, and it is widely available. Substitute finely julienned crisp cucumbers plus bits of dried NORI seaweed, or try rinsed sweet or dill pickles.

Okinawan sweet potato: Purple sweet potato.

Onaga: Japanese term for red snapper. The Hawaiian name is 'ula'ula. Red snapper has pink flesh. Substitute any pink or red snapper, such as 'ŌPAKAPAKA.

Ono: Hawaiian name for a large mackerel, also known as wahoo. Flesh has a white flaky texture. Substitute MAHIMAHI, halibut, cod, kingfish, swordfish.

Opah: Ocean moonfish.

'Ōpakapaka: Local deep-water fish. Its sweet, delicate flesh is always white when cooked. Runs from lean to fat, depending on the season.

'Opihi: Endemic limpets found on Hawai'i's rocky shores with strong wave action. Dangerous to gather. Substitute any edible limpet.

Oyster sauce: A thick brown sauce made from oysters, brine, and SHOYU. Used in many stir-fried dishes. Substitute regular or vegetarian forms.

P

Panko: Japanese coarse breadcrumbs used for crunchy deep-fried coatings. Substitute fine dry breadcrumbs.

Papaya: A tropical fruit with yellow or orange flesh and a shiny green or yellow skin. Substitute crenshaw melon to give similar color and texture but not same flavor.

Passion fruit: See LILIKO'I.

Peanut oil: It's ideal for frying and deep-frying. Substitute grape seed oil.

Pineapple: The fruit of a bromeliad plant originally native to Brazil. It is available year-round in Hawai'i. Substitute canned pineapple.

Pipikaula: Dried beef jerky.

Pohā: Hawaiian name for cape gooseberry; a tangy sweet fruit usually made into jams, jellies, sauces, and desserts.

Poi: A paste made from steamed, pounded TARO. Substitute unseasoned mashed potatoes thinned to a thick batter consistency.

Poke: Hawaiian word for slice; refers to a traditional Hawaiian dish of sliced raw fish, Hawaiian salt, seaweed, and chilies.

Portuguese sausage: A spicy pork sausage seasoned with onions, garlic, and pepper.

R

Red chili pepper flakes: Dried and crushed red chili peppers. Substitute any chili pepper, finely chopped and seeded.

Rice stick noodles: Rice vermicelli

Rock lobster: Also called spiny lobster with all the meat in the tail and no claws. Substitute any lobster meat.

S

Saimin: Local Japanese soup made of wheat egg noodles.

Sake: Slightly sweet Japanese rice wine. Substitute sherry.

Sambal oelek: This fiery-hot chili paste is a table condiment in Indonesia. Also known as hot Asian chili paste. Substitute any fiery-hot chili paste.

Sashimi: Very thin slices of fresh raw fish.

Sesame oil: A dense, flavorful oil pressed from SESAME SEEDS. If cold-pressed from untoasted seeds, it will be very clear and mild-flavored; if from toasted sesame seeds, it will be dark brown and strong-flavored.

Sesame seeds: Seeds of a flowering plant found throughout Eurasia and Africa with a distinctive nutty flavor. Substitute finely chopped toasted almonds.

Shallots: More like a garlic than an onion, with a head composed of one or two cloves and a mild onion flavor. Substitute green onion bulb.

Shiitake mushroom: Shiitakes have a woodsy, smoky flavor. If using the dried variety, soak in warm water for 30 minutes before using. Remove stems.

Shiso: Valued for its refreshing taste, it has beefsteak leaves. Substitute mint or basil.

Shoyu: A salty liquid made from fermented boiled soybeans, roasted barley or wheat, monosodium glutamate (MSG), and salt. Usually dark brown in color, it is the principal seasoning in Asian cooking and there are many varieties. Shoyu, the Japanese term, is the Hawaiʻi term for what is called SOY SAUCE on the Mainland. Substitute 3 parts Worcestershire sauce to 1 part water.

Soba noodles: Japanese buckwheat noodles, thin, and light brown in color, and eaten warm or cold. Substitute angel hair pasta.

Somen noodles: Delicate Japanese noodles made from hard wheat flour. Substitute vermicelli.

Soy sauce: See SHOYU.

Spiny lobster: See ROCK LOBSTER. Substitute any lobster.

Squid: When buying fresh squid, look for squid that are small and whole, with clear eyes and an ocean (but not fishy) smell. Squid must be carefully cooked so it does not become rubbery. Frequently sold as CALAMARI. Substitute octopus.

Sriracha hot sauce: U.S.-made hot sauce from sun-ripened chili peppers, vinegar, garlic, sugar, and salt. Similar to the hot sauces of Vietnam and Thailand.

Sushi: A vinegar-sugar mixture rice served with raw or poached seafood, vegetables, sliced omelet, and other tasty morsels. Some sushi are wrapped in NORI.

Sweet potato: The orange-colored edible root of a tropical American vine often confused with the yam, which can be used as a substitute.

T

Tako: Japanese word for octopus. Islanders tend to say "tako" or HEʻE rather than "octopus." Tako can be difficult to cook, as it can become rubbery if not handled correctly. Don't overcook. It is sometimes tenderized. Substitute SQUID.

Taro: A nutritious, starchy tuber used for making POI, the traditional Hawaiian staple. More than 200 taro varieties are grown worldwide. It cannot be eaten raw, as raw taro is full of irritating oxalic acid crystals which dissolve when boiled or steamed. Substitute any firm-fleshed potato.

Tempura: Battered and deep-fried seafood or vegetables.

Teriyaki: A marinade or sauce, generally consisting of SHOYU, sugar, GINGER, and garlic. Substitute mixture of shoyu, SAKE or sherry, sugar, and ginger.

Thai basil: A variety of basil grown in Thailand. Substitute sweet basil.

Ti leaves: The leaves of a woody plant in the agave family grown throughout Polynesia. Used to wrap foods before cooking them in an IMU. Substitute BANANA LEAVES, corn husks, or aluminum foil.

Tobiko: Flying fish roe. Substitute any fish roe.

Tofu: Japanese name for a bland-flavored soybean curd that can be custard-like in texture (soft tofu) or quite firm. The firm and extra-firm forms are generally used in stir-frying or deep-frying.

U

Uku: Hawaiian name for the gray snapper.

ʻUlu: Hawaiian name for BREADFRUIT.

W

Wasabi: Pungent root with an extremely strong, sharp flavor. Popular Japanese horseradish condiment. Substitute hot dry mustard.

White pepper: Made from pepper berries picked when very ripe and completely red. The peppercorns are then dried. Their flavor is much milder than that of black peppercorns. Substitute black pepper.

Wok: A versatile round-bottomed pan used in Chinese cookery with and without a cover for stir-frying, steaming, boiling, braising, and deep-frying. Similar to the karhai, used in Indian cooking.

Won bok: Chinese or Napa cabbage. Substitute savoy or other green cabbage.

Won ton wrappers: Also called spring-roll wrappers. Flat, thin squares of wheat dough, used to wrap various tasty fillings. Available fresh or frozen. Refrigerate.

Recipe Index

People & Places Index

My crew:
Creative, passionate, and all *Maui!*

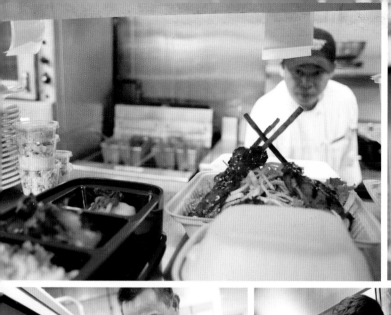

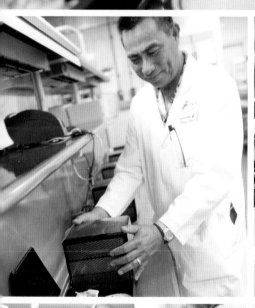

About the Authors

Chef Tylun Pang
Director of Food & Beverage and Executive Chef, The Fairmont Kea Lani, Maui

Fortunate to be Hawai'i-born, Chef Pang has grown up with many cultural influences. This diversity reflects in his style of cooking. The emphasis on using fresh fish and local ingredients from sustainable resources adds to a unique cuisine that nurtures the aloha spirit inside you.

Tylun Pang, Director of Food & Beverage and Executive Chef of The Fairmont Kea Lani, Maui, oversees banquet and catering operations, as well as the resort's three restaurants including Kō plantation inspired cuisine, Luana Lounge and Caffe Ciao gourmet bakery and deli. Pang began his career in 1974 and brings many years of experience to his position. He was presented The Mayor's Award in Culinary Excellence for the County of Maui in 2005. He currently serves on the advisory board of the Maui Community College's Maui Culinary Academy.

Gail Ainsworth, kama'āina resident of Maui, has researched and written about her island for 20 years. Her most well-known publication is the award-winning *Maui Remembers: A Local History,* which was published in 1994 and is still in print. Her other publications include magazine articles, Website articles, a book review in the *Hawaiian Journal of History* and three indexes to *The Maui News* which cover 1900-1973. She worked as a Hawaiiana/reference librarian at Maui Community College for 29 years. She loves to eat and describes herself as a "local foodie," making her an ideal person to write about local restaurants and recipes.

238

Index